Voices of a City Ma

Full details of all our other publications can be found on http://www.multilingual-matters.com, or by writing to Multilingual Matters, St Nicholas House, 31–34 High Street, Bristol BS1 2AW, UK.

Voices of a City Market

An Ethnography

Adrian Blackledge and Angela Creese

MULTILINGUAL MATTERS

Bristol • Blue Ridge Summit

DOI https://doi.org/10.21832/BLACKL5099
Library of Congress Cataloging in Publication Data
A catalog record for this book is available from the Library of Congress.
Names: Blackledge, Adrian, author. | Creese, Angela, author.
Title: Voices of a City Market: An Ethnography/Adrian Blackledge and Angela Creese.
Description: Blue Ridge Summit, PA : Multilingual Matters, [2019] | Includes bibliographical
    references. | Description based on print version record and CIP data provided by publisher;
    resource not viewed.
Identifiers: LCCN 2019010662 (print) | LCCN 2019018895 (ebook) | ISBN 9781788925105 (pdf) |
    ISBN 9781788925112 (epub) | ISBN 9781788925129 (Kindle) | ISBN 9781788925099 (hbk: alk.
    paper) | ISBN 9781788925082 (pbk: alk. paper)
Subjects: LCSH: Markets–Social aspects. | Sociolinguistics.
Classification: LCC HF5470 (ebook) | LCC HF5470 .B53 2019 (print) | DDC 381/.1–dc23
LC record available at https://lccn.loc.gov/2019010662

British Library Cataloguing in Publication Data
A catalogue entry for this book is available from the British Library.

ISBN-13: 978-1-78892-509-9 (hbk)
ISBN-13: 978-1-78892-508-2 (pbk)

Multilingual Matters
UK: St Nicholas House, 31-34 High Street, Bristol BS1 2AW, UK.
USA: NBN, Blue Ridge Summit, PA, USA.

Website: www.multilingual-matters.com
Twitter: Multi_Ling_Mat
Facebook: https://www.facebook.com/multilingualmatters
Blog: www.channelviewpublications.wordpress.com

The policy of Multilingual Matters/Channel View Publications is to use papers that are natural,
renewable and recyclable products, made from wood grown in sustainable forests. In the manufac-
turing process of our books, and to further support our policy, preference is given to printers that
have FSC and PEFC Chain of Custody certification. The FSC and/or PEFC logos will appear on
those books where full certification has been granted to the printer concerned.

Typeset by R. J. Footring Ltd, Derby, UK
Printed and bound in the UK by Short Run Press Ltd.
Printed and bound in the US by NBN.

It never ceases to amaze me how interesting everyday life really is
Svetlana Aleksievich

Oh, your temple of art echoes the yelling of the traders
Bertolt Brecht

Photographs about nothing very much, which describe human life
Dorothea Lange

We have to learn to trust the poet, trust ourselves, and trust that the poet has trusted us
Don Paterson

To market, to market to buy a fat pig / Home again, home again, jiggety jig
Anon.

For our mothers

Contents

PART ONE

Meat

Characters

THE PRAGMATIC BUTCHER migrated from China 13 years ago. He is co-proprietor of a butcher stall in the city market. He is married to THE GENIAL BUTCHER. They have three young children. THE PRAGMATIC BUTCHER is a version of THE PRAGMATIC BUTCHER in Part Two.

THE GENIAL BUTCHER migrated from Malaysia 12 years ago. Her parents are Chinese. She is co-proprietor of a butcher stall in the city market. She is married to THE PRAGMATIC BUTCHER. They have three young children. THE GENIAL BUTCHER is a version of THE GENIAL BUTCHER in Part Two.

THE RESEARCHER is committed to her profession as an ethnographer. She migrated from China 10 years ago.

THE DOCUMENTARY NOVELIST writes accounts of ongoing life. She values the polyphonic novel for its blend of documentary material and literary art. THE DOCUMENTARY NOVELIST is a version of Svetlana Aleksievich.

THE DRAMATURG believes in a theatre for the people that allows the audience to reflect critically on human life. He is concerned with the relationship between theatre and politics. THE DRAMATURG is a version of THE DRAMATURG in *The Messingkauf Dialogues* by Bertolt Brecht.

THE ENTREPRENEUR is a patron of, and an investor in, the arts. He prides himself on spotting new talent and promoting success.

THE PHOTOGRAPHER proposes that photography can be used to create a new repository of cultural history. She is drawn to the power of the mundane. THE PHOTOGRAPHER is a version of Dorothea Lange.

THE POET responds to the rhythm and rhyme of everyday life. For him, poetry has the ability to distil experience and to reveal the human condition. THE POET is a version of Don Paterson.

THE PROFESSOR seeks to represent the complexity of human life through research. She has an interest in the relationship between ethnography and the arts.

Nine wooden chairs face inwards in a circle. On the chairs sit THE PRAGMATIC BUTCHER, THE GENIAL BUTCHER, THE DRAMATURG, THE DOCUMENTARY NOVELIST, THE ENTREPRENEUR, THE PHOTOGRAPHER, THE POET, THE PROFESSOR *and* THE RESEARCHER. THE RESEARCHER *has brought coffee and croissants. She hands round the cups of coffee. She places the plate of croissants on the floor in the centre of the circle.*

3

THE RESEARCHER

THE ENTREPRENEUR. I want to explore the question of what it has been like to be a research participant. *[To* THE GENIAL BUTCHER *and* THE PRAGMATIC BUTCHER*]* How has it been for you? I mean having microphones clipped to you, and video-cameras pointed at you, with these two *[gestures to* THE RESEARCHER *and* THE PROFESSOR*]* writing down every single word you utter, and describing every action you perform. Was it, I mean, intrusive? Did it feel like you had been put under the microscope in a scientific experiment? Were you like rats in the laboratory? Was it uncomfortable?

THE GENIAL BUTCHER. It was all right. As it happened, our third baby arrived the day before the field work was due to begin, so I wasn't much involved to start with. But it was fine. After a while you forget about the fact that the researchers are there, and get on with your work. I was sorry that the baby coming at that time meant I couldn't do the university training and the qualification. I would have liked to learn more. But there was no way round that.

THE PRAGMATIC BUTCHER. Yes it was fine. It was a bit strange at first, especially with the voice recorder and the microphone. People did ask questions, but overall it was fine. No problem. If I needed to switch the recorder off I could, so whenever it was not appropriate to record I just did that. I suppose I wasn't all that keen to hand over my mobile phone to them so they could copy my social media messages and all that, but even then it was okay. I really only use the phone for taking orders.

THE ENTREPRENEUR. What I'm interested in is the question of your role as a character in the, well, if you like, the play, or the novel, or the ethnography. Do you feel that you were being directed, your lines written for you, and performed by you, that you were being constructed as a character in that way? Did you feel as if you were being directed to behave in particular ways by the research team? How did that seem to you?

THE PRAGMATIC BUTCHER. I'm not sure that I understand the question. I did what they said, they told me to be myself, they said don't do anything different from normal. That's what I did. I carried on selling meat as usual, talking to customers, going about my business.

THE ENTREPRENEUR. So they did say that to you at least. To that extent you were directed. They gave you that direction, telling you what to do. Did they want you to behave in certain prescribed ways?

THE PRAGMATIC BUTCHER. No, no. They said just do what you normally do.

THE PROFESSOR. Oh come on, explaining the research project doesn't constitute directing the action, or creating a character. As a research team we had to give some sort of context to the butchers. We talked to them about our research questions. You can't just say nothing. You have to have some kind of relationship with the character,

I mean the participant. There has to be a dialogue between the research team and the subject of the research. We didn't ask them to do anything other than be themselves.

THE RESEARCHER. That is what I was going to say. As researchers, we didn't create the butchers, or their customers, or the other stall-holders. They were what they were, and we recorded what we saw and heard. We did not make any kind of intervention. We were there, we observed everything, and we recorded everything. But the life of the market would have gone on exactly the same if we had not been there.

THE ENTREPRENEUR. You're arguing that your presence as researchers made no difference at all? That really can't be true. Everything makes a difference. Everything changes something. The butchers clearly were under observation, and they must have behaved differently because there you were, writing in your notebook, and because you were recording them with a digital voice recorder. They must have changed the way they spoke, because they were very well aware that every syllable would be transcribed and scrutinised.

THE POET. I don't think it's inevitable. People usually forget about the recorder after about ten or fifteen minutes, then occasionally remember again, maybe to check that it is still on.

THE RESEARCHER. It is certainly possible that the butchers were aware of the recorder and that they spoke differently because of it. But that doesn't invalidate the material we collected. It only means that there was an element of performativity in the butchers' interactions. If anything, that makes the data more valid, rather than less so. If they remembered that they were being recorded they were possibly more themselves rather than less.

THE GENIAL BUTCHER. I don't remember doing anything different. We just carried on as normal.

THE RESEARCHER. Yes, that is how it seemed to me. You carried on your everyday lives.

THE DRAMATURG. I'm not so sure. You don't feel that, having now represented the voices of the butchers as text, having textualised and recontextualised them, made films about them and whatever else, you don't feel that this process makes them into newly created characters? That is, in some sense you are their authors?

THE RESEARCHER. It is still their voices. It is still them. We are taking authentic material, transcribing it, analysing it and presenting it. Are we creating new characters? No, I don't think so. Are we giving voice to those whose voices are normally unheard and unrepresented? I think yes, I think that is what we are doing.

THE PROFESSOR [*to* THE ENTREPRENEUR]. I know where you're coming from. It's both, I suppose. Recording what's there and making something new. It's a kind of dynamic.

There is a sense in which whenever you represent a voice, you are creating a new character, constructing someone quite new. The recontextualisation of the voice can never be the same as the original voice.

THE PRAGMATIC BUTCHER. What, so when you record me selling a kilogram of chicken feet you are making me into someone else? Really? I have to say I think that's bollocks.

THE ENTREPRENEUR. That's interesting. Do you want to say a bit more about that?

THE PRAGMATIC BUTCHER. Look, I'm a working man. For a living I chop pigs into pieces, remove their guts, their entrails, the whole lot, and I sell the meat and offal for a few pennies so I can put bread on the table and provide for my kids. That's it. That's the long and short of it. I'm happy to be part of their research project because they're paying me, and anyway it's something different from the usual stuff. It makes a change. But I'm a butcher selling meat and offal. It's as simple as that.

THE DRAMATURG. But you must not make the mistake of believing that you are free of the structures in society which govern us all, the discourses which produce us as entities. After all, you look like a butcher, you sound like a butcher, you smell like a butcher, because you have learned how to be a butcher. You have been produced by the history of butchery. And the market has constructed you into becoming and being a butcher. You are a corollary of the discourses of the market.

THE GENIAL BUTCHER. A what, a corollary? That's just not, I mean, it's too simplistic, surely? What about agency? Are you saying we are nothing but the product of our environment? We were in catering before. What does that mean? Your job doesn't define you entirely. We are not only butchers. We are individuals with lives. I am a woman, a mother, a wife, a multilingual, Malaysian, Chinese, British, feminist and a hundred other categorisations which are not reducible to a corollary of the discourses of the market. We might be the product of our time and place in history, but we are more than the discourse of the market.

THE PRAGMATIC BUTCHER. I learned how to be a butcher, for sure, because I had to. I had to learn how to cut the meat, find out how much I needed and how to sell it. I had to learn how to be civil to people when it was the last thing I felt like doing. I had to learn how to make a living from buying and selling. That isn't some abstract, academic exercise. It's about feeding your family, putting food on the table at the end of the day.

THE RESEARCHER. I have to say that I agree with you. Although I am originally from China, I have lived here for a long time. I studied in this country and I have worked here. My friends are mostly local, but some are from further afield. I don't speak Mandarin very often, unless I call home. Technically Mandarin is my own language but something about it isn't mine anymore. I would call myself an academic. I have worked as a researcher in universities over the last few years. Of course, being Chinese was really important in securing my role as a researcher on the project. The research team wanted to explore migrants and the language of workplaces. I repeatedly spent time observing the Chinese butcher's stall in the market. I spent many days conducting an ethnographic study in the market, standing around with the professor, watching people as they interacted with the butchers, and chatting to them about all sorts of things when business was quiet. At the end of each day I would type up my field notes for later analysis. In the project I am the Chinese researcher. Sometimes I feel that I am treated as if all I bring to the project is speaking Chinese. But a Chinese speaker is not all I am.

THE PROFESSOR. I'm not sure it's fair to say that you are treated as if all you bring to the project is speaking Chinese. We needed to recruit someone who could speak and understand Chinese languages, of course, but more than that we wanted to work with someone who was able to establish good relationships with participants, work easily in a range of contexts, be independent, contribute to analysis from an insider's point of view. Actually our intention was to recruit a researcher of Chinese heritage who had lived in this country all their lives. But as it turned out, your background was ideal, because you shared much of the migration history of the research participants. It meant you could offer the perspective of an insider.

THE RESEARCHER. But that's just it. I don't have an insider's point of view. Just the fact that I am from China doesn't make me an insider. In fact in some ways it is irrelevant.

THE ENTREPRENEUR. But you have been in this country for about the same number of years as the two butchers. You must surely feel that you share that experience with them, the migrant journey, the becoming, belonging and being, the integration into society. You have that same hinterland to draw on. Don't you?

THE RESEARCHER. That's only part of it. How much do you share with everyone else who has lived in this country for the last fifty years? Are you all the same? Do you have everything in common? Do you choose to be characterised as a white, male, middle-class, fifty-something has-been? As a more-or-less liberal but too-pompous-to-listen intellectual who would have produced the perfect piece of theatre if only circumstances had not been against him? Do you share this experience with all the other white, male, middle-class, fifty-something has-beens? Or are you able to position yourself in other ways because you have the power to do so? Who gets to choose?

[THE ENTREPRENEUR *takes his coffee outside the circle and stands with his back to the others*]

THE DOCUMENTARY NOVELIST. We should be civil to each other, even if we don't agree. Mud-slinging isn't going to help. I mean, I can see your point. No one wants to be just a stereotype.

THE POET. Of course there must be as many differences between you as there are similarities.

THE RESEARCHER. It irritates me, the way researchers are treated by universities. Can I get a permanent contract? No. Can I get a mortgage? No. I go beyond what I am supposed to do, transcribing hundreds of hours of recordings, working on my own, most of it never used for anything. I mean, do you know how long it takes? Thousands of hours of listening to people buy meat. It was a great project, I enjoyed it, don't get me wrong. It was interesting from start to finish. But I work harder than anyone. I do everything I'm asked to. And so what? Will it get me another job when this is over? No way.

THE PROFESSOR. I am completely sympathetic to that, but that's the system. It's what you bought into when you took the job. Researchers are very rarely able to find permanent or extended contracts. That's just the way it is. I'm sure you knew that.

THE RESEARCHER. But that doesn't make it all right. You can't just accept things the way they are because they are the way they are. It isn't right.

THE PHOTOGRAPHER

THE PHOTOGRAPHER [*to THE RESEARCHER*]. When you say most of the stuff you produce is never looked at, or never used, or whatever, what do you mean? Who decides what goes forward and what ends up on the cutting-room floor? What is the process?

THE RESEARCHER. In the first instance, it was me going through the audio-recordings. But there is far too much stuff to transcribe; you couldn't possibly make sense of it all. We wrote more than a hundred thousand words of field notes in note pads in the market, then typed them up in the evenings. That all had to be analysed and discussed in meetings. Then you start making audio-recordings, and transcribing those, and it's endless. To start with, I was going to transcribe everything, but it was just too much. I mean, it takes me twelve to fifteen hours to transcribe one hour of recorded material from the market stall, and we had, what, nearly a hundred hours, and then you think of the audio-recordings the butchers did at home, another fifty hours or something like that. And the recordings made on the market stall are not always easy to listen to. You have a lot of extraneous noise, a lot of clatter and shouting, and several people talking at once. You have to listen to the same episode over and over again to get it right.

THE PRAGMATIC BUTCHER. And there are people speaking different languages. You don't always know whether they are speaking their language, or speaking English with an accent. I find that.

THE RESEARCHER. So I quickly gave up on transcribing everything. You don't need it all though. How many different ways are there of saying half a kilogram of pork mince and three pig feet?

THE PROFESSOR. So to make the workload more manageable we agreed that you would listen to all the recordings, select the episodes which would be transcribed, and bring the transcripts to meetings for analytical discussion.

THE POET. You did all the selection of episodes yourself?

THE RESEARCHER. Yes, that's what happened in the end. But of course it's never as simple as that. The market is a noisy, busy place; you can't always hear what is being said on the recording, so you have to go over and over it. Quite a lot of it is in Mandarin, which is fine, but there's extra work in transcribing the Chinese, then producing the English translation. And then when the interaction includes Cantonese, Hakka, Fujianese and so on, it's challenging because I am not really up to speed with all those languages. People sometimes assume that because you are Chinese you can speak all the different Chinese languages and varieties. It isn't the case. I did my best, but sometimes we had to get help from elsewhere, and that caused delays.

THE PROFESSOR. You did a fabulous job though, selecting and transcribing the episodes for analysis. We definitely couldn't have done that without you.

THE POET. It's a big job.

THE RESEARCHER. It was fine, but yes, it was labour intensive. And again, I could understand the Mandarin, but not all the Chinese languages. I had to listen to all the recordings, keep track of which episodes might be interesting to transcribe, then start work on transcription. There were always deadlines, always another meeting round the corner. I had to make quick decisions about which episodes to transcribe. Of course, the parts of recordings I decided not to transcribe were not lost. We didn't discard the recordings, but there was less chance that we would come back to them once they had not been selected for transcription. It was very time consuming. I found myself working evenings and weekends just to present the material on time. I mean, the meetings themselves were incredibly rich, going through the transcripts together and doing this kind of collaborative analysis. It was really illuminating. But preparing the transcripts was demanding in terms of time.

THE PHOTOGRAPHER. This question of what ends up on the cutting-room floor, the metaphor itself tells you, it resonates with my own process of curation. I take far more photographs than ever find their way into an exhibition or a book. And I think the decision-making must be similar. Like you, I am trying to select examples which, while they are not necessarily representative or typical, tell something of the human condition in a particular time and place.

THE RESEARCHER. I can see that, yes, there are similarities. And that process of selection is subjective as well as scientific.

THE PHOTOGRAPHER. The question we grapple with is, how do you tell others about what you think is worth telling? That you have either discovered, or uncovered, or learned, or been endowed with in one way or another, what you think is meaningful? You try. You find your way. And no one can assure you when you've been successful and when you haven't. You never really know that. But that's what the job is. You have to have confidence in your own judgements, your own decision-making. It's better if you can share that process with others, but usually there isn't time. You have to get on and do it.

THE RESEARCHER. Yes, yes, I see that. It's the same for me. The thing is that everything you are collecting, or producing, is ordinary, everyday stuff. So how do you distinguish between what is too ordinary to be of interest and what is ordinary enough to be fascinating. This service encounter in which a customer buys two pig stomachs, against that service encounter in which a different customer buys two chickens. Which do we keep and which do we discard? And why? Especially as we don't fully understand what might be the significance of an interaction until we have examined it several times in some detail. Sometimes extraordinary things come to the surface when you look closely at what seems to be the most innocuous example.

THE PHOTOGRAPHER. What I want to create, or to present in the photographs, and you might feel the same about what you are doing, is the essence of a case, the universality of a situation, not the circumstance. And when I go back to the photographs after some time, some things are better than I knew. I stop short at some, and look and look at them. It's similar to what you are saying. When I look again at them, look more carefully, I feel that isn't my photograph, I think what a great capturing of something that was.

THE RESEARCHER. That's it. I re-read field notes, or look again at transcripts, and feel that in a particular moment is captured a kind of truth. I can be astonished by the richness of the most ordinary encounter. You sometimes see clearly just exactly how people get along, despite their apparent differences. You start to see exactly how that process works. It really is a kind of truth.

THE PROFESSOR. I don't know that I would say truth necessarily, but something that is meaningful. We should be careful of saying that we have encountered or discovered the truth.

THE POET. All right. But whether you call it truth, or essence, or whatever other metaphor we come to, surely we are seeking to create something that is a distillation of the human condition, or at least a fundamental representation of the condition of humanity at a certain point in time and space. We strive towards something like that, don't we?

THE PHOTOGRAPHER. I would like to produce an exhibition so that people's minds might be stirred, not by the variety of things that I have looked at, but by the immense variety and richness of human life. But having said that, this is not the final step at all. This is sort of discovering what the core of the work is about. I'm sure that this idea takes not only working out, but some reworking. I've gone through this kind of a process before, but I have always, most of the time, done it alone. Working with other people, even talking with other people, provides a wealth of perspectives which you lose when you are working on your own.

THE RESEARCHER. Making these selections alone is hard for you, but for me, a junior member of a team, I was always anxious that I was making the wrong decisions. I was always anxious. So I always selected too many examples as a kind of insurance policy. If I didn't know whether to select this example or that example, I chose them both.

THE PHOTOGRAPHER. For me the pictures I choose to display suggest possibilities. I'm not doing it in terms of achievement. I feel it in terms of possibility, provocation, and I'd like to give it a push, just a slight push. What I feel is needed is a new repository of cultural history which focuses on the development of cities. The purpose of such a repository would not be to make the kind of picture that illustrates concepts that have already formed in people's minds, in order to prop up a popular understanding. It should be based on personal, direct exposure to what is really there, focusing not on the bizarre or the spectacular, but producing photographs about nothing very much, which describe human life.

THE PROFESSOR. The nothing very much which describes human life. That's it. You could say exactly that about our observations in the meat market. Nothing spectacular or bizarre, but observing the everyday business of people buying and selling meat. Yes, you are right, it describes human life.

THE PHOTOGRAPHER. For me, the assignment is to see what is really there, what it looks like, and in so doing to reveal the underpinning human condition. There you have it again, the human condition. Such observation is necessarily incomplete, unfinalised, and raises questions rather than providing answers. The viewer of these photographs of what I am calling nothing very much would say, oh yes, I know what she meant, I never thought of it, I never paid attention to it. Calling attention to the mundane, the everyday, the familiar, enables people to see as if for the first time something they had passed by a thousand times without comment.

THE RESEARCHER. Calling attention to the mundane. I suppose that's exactly what we are doing. Calling attention to the mundane. I like that.

THE PROFESSOR. What's that?

THE RESEARCHER. What she says. Calling attention to the mundane, the everyday, the familiar, inviting the reader, or the audience, to see as if for the first time. You could say finding the extraordinary in the ordinary. Or if not the extraordinary, which might be pushing it too far, at least discovering what may be revealed in the ordinary. I think that's what it is.

THE PHOTOGRAPHER. Paying attention to nothing very much, representing everyday human life, and so representing the human condition.

THE PROFESSOR. The nothing very much to which we call attention includes the voices of people in the market. And of course it's more than voices. It's also the way people walk, stand and sit, the way they tilt their heads, the gaze of their eyes, the shrug of their shoulders, the movement of their hands and fingers, their smile or frown, all are part of communication in human life, and part of the human condition. As such, the body is a resource for communication. And beyond that, the body is the vehicle, or the conduit for communication. Those metaphors don't really work. I mean that the body is entirely integral to communication. You see that more explicitly in the market than anywhere else. People really communicate with their bodies. And the more we look at what happens in the market, the more clearly we can see that communication generally is about the body.

THE PHOTOGRAPHER. That is evident in the photographs as well. In fact, photography is an ideal medium through which to observe how people's bodies are essential to communication. The photographs I took of migrants in the United States, very often people with little to fall back on, sometimes with nowhere to go. What was powerful was the sense of the body. It tells so much. A person's history is inscribed in their body.

THE PROFESSOR. That is exactly what we have found in our work. That sense of history, biography, identity, all manifested in the body. It can be difficult to evidence, but it is there. The way people move their bodies is inscribed over generations.

THE POET. This is something that poetry can capture. History is embodied in the individual. Poetry has the capacity to describe that intense detail of how the individual looks, how the individual feels.

THE PHOTOGRAPHER. One day I was working and it came to me. The deprived and the dislocated, and then another word came to me, the rootless, and helpless. And then the phrase that's used by, I think, the sociologists use it, the walking wounded. After all this austerity. There's another phrase that's in my mind: the last ditch. The last ditch.

THE RESEARCHER. Yes, all of that is there in the market. But it isn't all last ditch, even where there is poverty. That seems too gloomy, too apocalyptic. There is also the conviviality of people getting on together despite everything. It's inspiring.

THE ENTREPRENEUR [from outside the circle]. Oh yes, here we go again. Why don't you try living in poverty, and then come back and tell us it's inspiring.

THE RESEARCHER. There is poverty and poverty, it's true, but I'm only a humble researcher myself. Anyway, that's not what I mean. It's the conviviality of the market I find inspiring. That sense that because everyone needs to get on together, they can, and in the main they do. You know?

THE PHOTOGRAPHER. That's what it is. And you do what you can to make visible and meaningful the human condition. That's about all we can do.

THE DOCUMENTARY NOVELIST

THE DOCUMENTARY NOVELIST. For me it is about voice. That is our window on the human condition. In some ways I would say that I am a human ear. When I walk down the street and catch words, phrases and exclamations, I always think – how many novels disappear without a trace. They just disappear into darkness. We haven't been able to capture the conversational side of human life. We don't appreciate it; we aren't surprised or delighted by it. But it fascinates me, and has made me its captive. I love how humans talk. I love the lone human voice. It is my greatest love and passion.

THE ENTREPRENEUR [*rejoining the circle and reclaiming his seat*]. Voice and action cannot be separated though. Voice alone is not sufficient. You also need the context. You need to have a sense of where the voice comes from, and why. A voice is never disembodied, floating around outside the social world.

THE POET. In the poem, context is everything. I am sometimes told that poetry is outside of social context, as if it has an ethereal existence of its own. But for me the opposite is the case. Poetry cannot exist without the social world. Poetry is, if anything, a distillation of social life, a reduction to its essential quality. Or reduction may be the wrong word. It's about finding the quintessence of an experience.

THE DOCUMENTARY NOVELIST. I am making no great claims. I listen to people's stories. They are stories about war, about starvation, about love, about unimaginable horrors. Some of the things I have heard should be heard by no one. At times they are too difficult to listen to.

THE PROFESSOR. So do you make a truth, a reality from the stories? What if the people you talk to are not telling the truth, and are just out to impress you, or they want to lead you up the garden path? How do you know they are telling you what they have really experienced? How can you separate reality from unreality, truth from untruth?

THE DOCUMENTARY NOVELIST. The stories have their own truth, which I reconstruct from the narrative. I have collected the history of human life bit by bit. The history of how it plays out in the human soul. I am drawn to that small space called a human being, a single individual. In reality, that is where everything happens. I am not in the business of saying this is truth, or that is untruth. The task is to find the essential truth in the narrative.

THE DRAMATURG. I see that. But I am not sure about the emphasis on the individual. What about the collective consciousness, the collective voice? Does that not have a greater truth?

THE DOCUMENTARY NOVELIST. I listen to the voice of the individual. I don't know. For decades it was all about the collective. The collective above all, for the greater good of the common project. In the end, I'm not sure what that achieved.

THE RESEARCHER. You say you reconstruct truth from the narrative? Are you saying it is not important whether the events in the narrative really occurred?

THE DOCUMENTARY NOVELIST. It is not that the events did not occur. We all share history. But there are different narratives. Those individual narratives are part of a shared history. They have their own truth, their own essence.

THE PROFESSOR. Can something be both true and untrue at the same time?

THE DOCUMENTARY NOVELIST. Yes, of course. In the detail of events some things will be misremembered, or even invented. Does that make the story less true? Not necessarily. There is still the truth of the human soul. It has always troubled me that the truth doesn't fit into one heart, into one mind, that truth is somehow splintered. There's a lot of it, it is varied, and it is strewn about the world. But the truth of the human soul is discoverable in the narrative.

THE RESEARCHER. How does that translate into research? Surely what we are searching for is the truth of people's lives, their lived experience. If truth and untruth coexist, and are equally valid, where does that leave us? There must be a point at which we have to say okay, this is true, this really happened and is part of someone's experience, and that is untrue and is an invention.

THE DOCUMENTARY NOVELIST. Perhaps the search for truth should include the search for untruth. What I collect is the everyday life of feelings, thoughts and words. I collect the life of my time. I'm interested in the history of the soul. The everyday life of the soul, the things that the big picture of history usually omits, or disdains. I work with missing history. I am often told, even now, that what I write isn't literature, it's a historical document. What is literature today? Who can answer that question? We live faster than ever before. Content ruptures form. Breaks and changes it. Everything overflows its banks: music, painting, photography, poetry, theatre – even words in documents escape the boundaries of the document. There are no borders between fact and fabrication. One flows into the other. This is true in research as much as in literature. Witnesses are not impartial. In telling a story, humans create, they wrestle time like a sculptor does marble. They are actors and creators.

THE DRAMATURG. So there is no border between fact and fiction?

THE DOCUMENTARY NOVELIST. For me it is not an important distinction. I'm interested in little people. The little, great people, is how I would put it, because suffering expands people. In my books these people tell their own little histories, and big history is told along the way. We haven't had time to comprehend what has happened to us, and is still happening to us; we just need to say it. To begin with, we must at least articulate what happened. We are afraid of doing that; we're not up to coping with our past. That is why I say it is about voice. Giving voice to what is happening to us.

THE GENIAL BUTCHER. I can see what you mean. There is no truth now. Everything is post-truth. If we have political leaders whose main currency is untruth, what value does truth have? If we have sections of the media which have invented stories for the longest time, what does truth mean? We have to live with both truth and untruth. We have to accept that they coexist.

THE DOCUMENTARY NOVELIST. The stories change because the storytellers change. I was writing history through the stories of its unnoticed witnesses and participants. They had never been asked anything. No one had ever wanted to know. What do people think? We don't really know what people think about great ideas. Right after a war, a person will tell the story of one war. A few decades later, it is like a different war. Something changes, because she has folded a whole life into those memories. An entire self. How she lived during those years, what she read, saw, who she met. What she believes in. Finally, whether she is happy or not. Documents are living creatures – they change as we change. What you are calling research is no different. Your field notes, your transcripts, your recordings change as you change. Nothing stays the same, because we change.

THE RESEARCHER. Oh God! Don't tell me that we have to start again and reanalyse everything!

THE DOCUMENTARY NOVELIST. That is not for me to say. What I can say is that, for me, the only way to represent the voices of the people I meet is to treat them equally, so that everyone's perspective is as valid as the next. The aim is to avoid the representation of dialogue and narration as finalised, or finished, so that the narrative comes as close as possible to life itself. This is not life as it is represented according to a coherent narrative, but life in its mere existence. It is continuous, ongoing life, which from the perspective of the subject is always in the process of becoming. Narrative is not fixed and stable. It changes as it is narrated.

THE POET. The same can be said of the lyric. Each reader or listener brings something new to the lyric, and in doing so changes it. The lyric is never the same again as when the poet laid down her pen. It alters as it finds its audience.

THE PHOTOGRAPHER. That is more or less what I was trying to say. Just as you curate the voices of the people you speak to, so I curate the images of the people I meet, and represent ongoing, everyday life. It is life in its dynamic state. Photographs are sometimes presumed to be the most static of media. But every time a photograph is viewed, it changes. There is always a relationship between the image and its viewer. And it is never finalised, never finished.

THE DOCUMENTARY NOVELIST. And what you end up with, what you curate, is characterised by a plurality of voices, each with equal rights and each with its own world, voices which combine but are not merged in the unity of the event. Each character, each voice, speaks in its own right rather than at the behest of the all-seeing author.

THE RESEARCHER. And so can we say something similar about research? Are the voices we collect similarly a plurality of consciousnesses, each with, what did you say, equal rights and each with its own world? Does each of the voices we collect in our material speak in its own right?

THE DOCUMENTARY NOVELIST. Absolutely, yes, yes. I can't see that there is a difference. I write documentary novels, you create ethnographies. You write documentary novels, I create ethnographies. Is there a difference?

THE PROFESSOR. That is exactly what we have come to realise. In ethnography, people's voices create their social world. Ethnography connects individuals whose completely different points of view might very well be at odds, and even clash, in real life. That is what ethnography can achieve – multiple perspectives which not only reflect, but also construct, the complexity of the social world.

THE GENIAL BUTCHER. You talk about voice, and voices, and, yes, I can see that. All kinds of voices in the market. We hear voices from everywhere. But you don't have to spend long in the market to see that communication is about more than voice. If people want something, they might not share a language, so they point to what they want. To show you how many they want, they hold up fingers. If they want it chopped, they make a chopping gesture. If they want the head off, they slash their throats with their hands. If they agree, they give a thumbs-up. They nod their head or shake their head. If they want to buy tongue, they point to their tongue. There are all kinds of ways of communicating that aren't actually about the voice as such.

THE PROFESSOR. Yes, exactly, you're absolutely right; it's that thing of the body being integral to communication. It's a good example of that.

THE DOCUMENTARY NOVELIST. For me, it is less about voices than about different perspectives on the world, different points of view. My own writing is precisely constructed as multiple perspectives, which often correspond to a multiplicity of coexisting, and sometimes directly competing, points of view.

THE DRAMATURG. It's about freeing yourself from the consciousness of the author, which traditionally binds together plot, style, tone and narrative. Adopting new principles for an artistic combination of elements and for the construction of the whole. There must be more than one way of understanding the world. This is essential to a conception of collective art. It is a fundamental foundation of the democratic theatre.

THE RESEARCHER. I am not about to accept that we throw out the hard labour of ethnographic data collection and analysis, though. I am not ready to say that the voices in the market stem from an implied author, or that we can regard them as fictional. They are voices which are not finalised externally, but they do testify to everyday human life. They are real voices in the real social world. They are not the imaginings of a novelist sitting at the kitchen table with her laptop. We have been to the market and listened and looked, repeatedly, and over time. I am not going to give that away and turn it all over to fiction.

THE DOCUMENTARY NOVELIST. I can understand that. And for me, too, I have interviewed thousands of people, who told me the most harrowing stories. They cried as they spoke. But, in the end, I am not concerned so much with the facts of a case as with its universal qualities. For this reason, what I aim to do is to capture and represent the emotional history of an experience. Not every word needs to be transcribed faithfully. Or at least, it may be transcribed faithfully, but in the curation, in the placement of that narrative, some elements become salient and others less so. Some elements contain the emotional essence.

THE DRAMATURG. That is very grand, but I come back to the question of fact and fiction. If there is no threshold between them, if fact and fiction are effectively the same, instead of standing for hours in the market with her notebook and voice recorder, why doesn't the researcher stay at her kitchen table and make it all up? Why bother going out into the world at all? Have you got an answer to that?

THE DOCUMENTARY NOVELIST. Well, I would always argue for the importance of being present, of listening to what people say. It is the essential thing of being there. It is about restoring experience to those who have been deprived of the opportunity to tell about it. To do this, you do have to go out to people and listen to them. That is it more than anything. Listening to what they have to say and finding the truth in it. So, no, it is not a matter of making it up, or of writing fiction. It is about recovering people's truth by listening to their voice. It is also about curating that voice, making it powerful, so that it can be heard. That is all I hope to achieve.

THE GENIAL BUTCHER

THE RESEARCHER. What I want to say is that there is no good reason why people should not be able to share the same social space and rub along together. All right, we might look different from each other, and sound different, and we might have different trajectories, employment histories, family biographies, educational careers, economic backgrounds, speak different languages, and so on, but why do we assume that these differences should be a cause of tension, a cause of problems? If you look around the city, if you really get up close to people in contact, I just don't see that.

THE PHOTOGRAPHER. You can't take anything for granted, or make any assumptions. All you can do is look carefully. And when those tensions are absent, it is still worth attending to what is going on. If anything it is more important than ever to discover what people do to oil the wheels of human interaction when they come into contact with others who look and sound different from them. If we are able to do this we are some way down the road towards a view of difference which has a positive rather than a negative orientation.

THE RESEARCHER. Yes, that's exactly what I'm arguing for. It is crucial to examine how people negotiate everyday encounters, especially when they are from different backgrounds. If investigating how people get along in their everyday lives has long been a concern for social research, it is a question that becomes increasingly pressing when people experience increasing diversification of diversity, more variegated patterns of mobility, and the intensification of experiences of radical difference.

THE PROFESSOR. That's a starting point, a starting point at the very least. I agree that assumptions about social categories can artificially construct social phenomena in ways which are potentially damaging, because they silence the voices of local actors. Much of the history of commentary on migration has focused on particular ethnic or national groups, their migration processes, community formation, trajectories of assimilation or integration, and patterns of transnationalism. People are spoken about as if they are no more than a category to which they are presumed to belong. The world is not so simple.

THE RESEARCHER. That's where the notion of what we sometimes call superdiversity comes in really useful. You're talking about multiple processes and effects of migration, leading to greater complexity in societies, as more people, from more varied cultural and linguistic backgrounds, subject to more varied conditions of mobility and legal status, come into regular contact with one another in expanding cities and towns. That is exactly what we see when we look at the market. There has never been so much mobility. But it's not only about numbers. The differences between people have become more pronounced, or at least the differences are more diverse. But the way some people talk about migration, you'd think migrants are all the same, when of course there are as many different types of migrants as there are migrants.

THE DOCUMENTARY NOVELIST. Is superdiversity just about migration though, or is it about everyone in a city or town, the complexity and unpredictability of what happens when people with different histories and trajectories come into contact? And that complexity is not just about the colour of your skin, or the language you speak, is it? It's about the totality of your biography and trajectory. Isn't that it?

THE PHOTOGRAPHER. Well, yes. I sometimes wonder where superdiversity begins and ends. So it is clear that a major capital city in western Europe is superdiverse. But what about the leafy suburbs, where people with money escape from the city? What about the village ten miles down the road? If some parts of the city are superdiverse, and some are not, where is the border between the two? Can we even use superdiverse as an adjective?

THE ENTREPRENEUR. I don't even know what the term means. What's supposed to be so super about superdiversity? Isn't it just another one of your academic buzzwords, a new name for the same old stuff? It seems to me that it's old wine in new bottles. I really don't see what's new about it.

THE POET. If you don't mind me saying so, I think that's a pretty crude characterisation. Old wine in new bottles? The world has moved on. If the demographics of societies change, and they certainly have, those of us who seek to understand societies need to change too.

THE ENTREPRENEUR. I don't buy it. There's nothing new in any of this. The global south has been superdiverse, if you're going to use that term, forever. For centuries you have had people of different backgrounds coming into contact. You can go back to the Romans and before the Romans. The Silk Road and all the other trading routes, east to west, north to south, the spice routes, the nomads following their herds, the great desert caravans, the Mongols, the fishing trails. But now a small group of north-west Europeans wants to claim that because there are more people from different places turning up on their doorstep they have discovered something called superdiversity. Some of these people don't mind erasing history with their so-called new ideas.

THE PROFESSOR. I don't think that's right. Superdiversity is far more than a descriptive term. It is a conceptualisation of people in contact which adopts specific orientations to difference. It isn't just about more diversity. It's about recognising that crude social categories have been used to limit the progress of multicultural societies. It is about a more sophisticated approach to understanding where we are and where we're going.

THE RESEARCHER. And the other thing is that you can't cling to the old thinking just because you weren't the first one to come up with something new. You have to let new ideas develop and go forward. Look at all the changes in the way people are communicating now. The proliferation of the digital world has completely changed the way we communicate. I mean billions of messages flying round the stratosphere every day. We can't just ignore that and pretend that we can go on as before. If we want to understand these phenomena, we need different analytical lenses, new ways of looking and listening.

THE ENTREPRENEUR. No, no, no. All this romantic, celebratory stuff about difference is too willing to ignore inequality. Are you saying that racism and discrimination are no longer relevant?

THE RESEARCHER. Absolutely not, absolutely not. Nobody is saying that. A way of understanding social difference which engages with complexity is precisely anti-racist. It is entirely and actively against discrimination and against prejudice. Countering inequality is the front and centre of superdiversity. But we are trying to move away from a view of the world which is based on simple structures in which the world is this or that, black or white. Racism must be countered wherever we see it. But such broad brush strokes are too simplistic. That kind of thinking is no longer useful. The world has changed and our thinking about the world has to change too.

THE PHOTOGRAPHER. That's right, that's right. We need to develop a more nuanced understanding of inequality. We need to look more closely and more carefully.

THE POET. It's a matter of how you think about it. You can't knock down every new term. You might have to be a bit patient and see whether it is picked up by the people who are planning the towns and cities of the future, the people who are at the practical end of it. If they find the term useful, I'm not sure that artists and academics have a right to stand in the way. Give it time.

THE ENTREPRENEUR. I can see that you are all determined to close ranks on this. [He stands up and walks to the outside of the circle, where he drinks his coffee with his back turned.]

THE PHOTOGRAPHER. But the other thing is the so-called migrant crisis. You hear it everywhere. On the news, from politicians, unquestioned, uncontested, migrant crisis, migrant crisis, migrant crisis. The only crisis is the failure of governments in the West, or do we say the global North, to plan for the arrival of large groups of mobile people, to make sure they arrive safely, and to provide resources to support them until they can support themselves. All of this movement of people was predictable. The war in Syria has been going on for years. We know about Yemen. We know where there is going to be drought and famine. We know where there is civil war. We know where people are chased from their homes by militia forces. We know where unemployment is high and wages low. We know that people want to live in a place where there is a chance the economy will be sufficient to support their family. This is not unpredictable. [To THE PRAGMATIC BUTCHER and THE GENIAL BUTCHER] I mean you are migrants, but you hardly constitute a crisis.

THE PRAGMATIC BUTCHER. No, but for us it has been a struggle, every step of the way, always a struggle. In some ways it still is a struggle. Things are better than they were, but it hasn't always been easy.

THE GENIAL BUTCHER. This thing about being a migrant. Are we migrants? What does it mean? We're here legally now, the same as everyone else. So why are we migrants? Who benefits from naming us as migrants? Can a person ever choose to stop being a migrant? We've lived here for more than ten years. We might look like migrants to you, but that doesn't mean that's how we feel. We're an ordinary family, doing what all families do. Who decides who is a migrant? When do we get to decide?

THE PROFESSOR. That's a good point. It's about agency and social positioning. That's a good example. And by observing interactions at the butcher's stall over time we can really begin to understand how people position you, and the extent to which you are able to position yourself.

THE PRAGMATIC BUTCHER. Well, I do understand that. I can see that you need to do detailed observation if you are to get a better comprehension of social life. But you know, we speak the same as everyone else, just normal, nothing special. We sell meat. It's everyday life. Honestly, I would have thought a university would have other things to study. But it's up to you.

THE PROFESSOR. Yes, that's exactly it, exactly that, everyday life, the life of the market, that's what interests us. We are interested in how people communicate when they have different backgrounds, different histories. What happens when people come into contact but they have different languages, different lives. By observing interactions in the market we can learn almost everything about social life.

THE RESEARCHER [to THE PRAGMATIC BUTCHER]. That is what we talked about at the start. We wanted you to be yourself, talk the way you normally talk. And that's what you did. We explained it all. You signed the forms to say you understood. And you did everything we asked of you, allowed us to observe you, to audio-record you, video-record you. You gave us your phone so we could copy your digital messages. You even audio-recorded yourself at home with your family. You say it is just normal, and nothing special, but that is ideal for us. It is that thing of calling attention to the mundane, to everyday life.

THE PRAGMATIC BUTCHER. Yes, it's not a problem of course; I'm happy to help. And the money comes in very handy.

THE ENTREPRENEUR [still standing outside the circle]. It is probably not essential that you understand everything. You don't need to be able to explain what is happening. In a sense, you are the point, you are the action. [He resumes his seat in the circle.]

THE DRAMATURG. Your voice, your actions, stand as representative of the working man, of labour, of the struggle to survive. People can see the action, hear the voices of the market. That's all that is needed.

THE PRAGMATIC BUTCHER. Which people?

THE DRAMATURG. You know, anyone reading the book, watching the film. It's almost like the theatre, a theatre of contradiction, a theatre for the people that allows the audience to reflect critically on life as it is, on human life, the life of the market. Not real life perhaps, but a representation of real life.

THE PRAGMATIC BUTCHER. A theatre of contradiction? A theatre for the people? If you say so.

THE PROFESSOR. Not that we are really arguing that what we have finally is reality. It is always a process. It is always a work in progress. The outcomes of the research are always emergent, always becoming. We are not saying that what we have is an ultimate and final truth of any kind. But we have something, something that stands apart from reality, apart from real life, and says this is about the human condition.

THE GENIAL BUTCHER. I don't know. A theatre of contradiction? A theatre for the people? If what you are representing in your so-called theatre is me down the wholesale market at four o'clock in the morning, two kids strapped to my back, stripping the guts out of pigs so we can sell them for pennies. If your theatre of contradiction includes cleaning the shit out of pig intestines before we can sell them on the market. If your theatre of contradiction is about the everyday racism of passers-by in the market hall. If your theatre of contradiction includes the market traders who blanked us for months and stole from our stall. If your theatre of contradiction tells of the constant threat of violence just because we happen to be Chinese. If your theatre of contradiction includes landlords and letting agents slamming doors in our faces. If your theatre of contradiction includes wholesalers ripping us off and doing deals with English butchers. If your theatre of contradiction includes being spat at in the street and told to get the next boat home. If your theatre of contradiction is getting conned out of our savings not once but twice because we trusted people. If your theatre of contradiction is a fight with meat cleavers on the floor of the market hall. Is that a real enough life for you? You can have your theatre of contradiction. You can have your theatre for the people. Meanwhile, we live it.

THE PRAGMATIC BUTCHER. Our lives are not an academic exercise. Nor do we live out our existence in a laboratory, to be poked and prodded and examined. We might be from another country, but we cry tears of salt like everyone else.

THE GENIAL BUTCHER. With all your doctorates and your degrees, your research grants and your publications, do you think you are really qualified to look at our lives and draw conclusions from them? Have you any idea what it is like to be a migrant in this country? Do you come anywhere near to understanding the life of a person of colour? Do you think your liberalism gives you the right to say this is the human condition, in all its hardship, in all its glory? You white people. You middle classes. You highly educated professors and artists, you ethnographers and photographers, you novelists and poets. Do you think that as long as you examine us closely enough you will come to know us, to make us out? Can you really see us from so far away? Really?

[Silence. They all look at the floor, and drink coffee. The PROFESSOR *takes a croissant from the plate in the centre of the circle]*

THE POET

THE POET. You have talked about representing human life, or human experience, or you might have said the human condition, through the photograph, through the novel, through documentary and through ethnographic research. But have you considered poetry? The poet and social scientist share commonalities in approach. Both ground their work in meticulous observation of the empirical world, are often reflexive about their work and experience, and have the capacity to foreground how subjective understanding influences their work. Poetry is able to distil experience in ways that may not be available in all media. So there may be a role for poetry in the representation of the human condition.

THE ENTREPRENEUR. As long as you don't run into the same issues as with the novel. Is the poem more truthful than prose fiction? There is no reason to suppose that it is. If anything, poetry by definition can take us further from the truth of experience into flights of the imagination.

THE PROFESSOR. But there you go again with the notion of the truth. I thought we had established that there is no single truth in human experience. We have to avoid suggesting that there is a single, unimpeachable truth, let alone that we have discovered what it is.

THE POET. I wouldn't necessarily argue that poetry is the crucible of truth, not by any means. I would say that it is in the enhancement of, and elaboration upon, social research outcomes that poetry has rich potential. Poetry can be an analytical or reflexive approach as well as a representational form. It is a form of enquiry which challenges notions of authenticity, acknowledges complexity and contests the single, sacred account of events. In that sense, poetry also has the ability to present more than a single view of the world.

THE ENTREPRENEUR. The last thing we need now is the introduction of terrible poetry into the equation! I'm tired of reading and listening to poor poetry that poses as research, and vice versa. If poetry is to be any use at all in social research it has to be decent quality. Poor poetry should never see the light of day.

THE POET. I wouldn't argue with that. At its best, poetry speaks to something universal, it clarifies the human condition in some part. But yes, if poetry is to contribute to social research it can do so only when it is good poetry.

THE ENTREPRENEUR. You agree then; it should be a good poem. It should have that quality that sets it apart. Doggerel will not do.

THE PROFESSOR. I think there's great potential in poetry for anthropologists to paint human life in ways that can prove difficult in ethnographic prose. The intensity of human experience is not always available in conventional ethnographic description. I do think there is potential there for poetry to go beyond what prose can do. Poetry has the ability to represent the rhythm and rhyme of social life. And of course it is more than representation. Poetry has the potential to extend experience, to go further than mere description.

THE RESEARCHER. But isn't there a risk that in doing so you move further and further away from your field notes, further and further away from the evidence? Shouldn't we retain the field notes themselves as primary data, rather than transfiguring them into something that might be more beautiful, but is probably less authentic? As we said before, the knowledge earned through ethnographic observation is hard won and should not be given away lightly.

THE POET. I don't see it as either or. Poetry has the potential to carry utterances away to meanings beyond themselves, to what humankind has known and experienced, to the human condition. The poem is not an end-point or a conclusion. It overlaps with other texts which represent everyday practice, rather than replacing them. Through an aesthetic sense, the poem reaches for an enhanced view, an expanded understanding, and complements other ways of constructing accounts of social life. To that extent, yes, poetry can do more than merely represent experience. It can also create meanings which were unreachable by other means.

THE PROFESSOR. I believe you can argue that field notes are as much a poetic as a scientific genre. The poet is faithful to external socio-historical experience, while reaching beyond the limits of research material to a sense of aesthetics that enhances understandings of the social world. It is about bringing together the aesthetic, the emotional and the scientific. The gulf between science and art is an artificial one.

THE ENTREPRENEUR. I maintain that poems which respond to research must first be good poems in and of themselves. Poetry has potential to detract from the research if the quality is not attended to.

THE DOCUMENTARY NOVELIST. It's a fair point, but who is going to determine what is a good poem and what is not? Isn't it a subjective judgement? Doesn't the question of taste come into it?

THE POET. Yes. But this kind of evaluation, the question of whether a poem is of sufficient quality or not, is made all the time in the world of poetry publishing and in poetry competitions. Poets live in the real world. They don't expect any old rubbish to be acceptable just because the words don't come up to the edge of the page. In fact, poets jealously guard the quality of the poem. The notion that there is some poetic muse on hand to provide a lightning bolt of inspiration is very much misguided. Good poetry comes into being through blood, sweat and tears. It is ninety-nine per cent perspiration and one per cent inspiration. If inspiration ever does turn up you had better be working. Poetry is hard labour.

THE PRAGMATIC BUTCHER. It is? Any time you want to swap with me and haul a dozen pig carcasses from the wholesale market at six o'clock in the morning, then cut them up into bellies, chops and steaks, take out the hearts, stomachs, livers and intestines, and stand in the draughty market all day flogging them, then clear up the mess until six thirty in the evening, any time you want to swap with me I'll do the hard labour of knocking out a few verses for you.

THE POET. Okay, fair enough. There's hard labour and hard labour.

THE PHOTOGRAPHER. But isn't there a place for poetry that is exploratory, that is trying to push beyond what conventional ethnographic writing can achieve, even though it may not tick all the boxes of what constitutes a good poem? What if an attempt to write in a more emotionally intense register reveals the human condition in ways that remain concealed in a more descriptive mode? Isn't there something about poetry as rough process rather than always having to be a polished product? Poetry has the potential to bridge subject areas; it has been used in disciplines such as anthropology, education, urban geography, nursing, psychology and social work. Poetry is to an extent shaped by the anthropological experience, as the poet reflects on experiences and reframes them through poetry.

THE POET. I agree that poetry has great potential to represent human experience. It is a naturally occurring mode of human speech. The effects we call 'poetic' occur when speech is made under two conditions: urgency and shortness of time. Language behaves in a material way and, placed under the dual pressures of emotional urgency and temporal constraint, it will reveal its structure and grain. Under such conditions language becomes rhythmic, lyrical, and original. That lyricism, that originality, is what makes it poetry. That rhythm. Poetry reveals the underlying metrical and intonational regularity of language, and its tendency to pattern its sounds. It reveals the rhythms that dominate the natural phrase and sentence lengths of language, and its narrative and argumentative episodes. The butcher's stall is an environment in which urgency and temporal constraint are salient features. There is little time. Things move quickly. Service encounters can last a matter of a few seconds.

THE PRAGMATIC BUTCHER. But what goes on is everyday buying and selling. It is not really the stuff of poetry.

THE POET. Poetry exaggerates or at least calls attention to features already present or latent in speech. It emerges naturally from speech as the immediate consequence of emotional urgency. Our desire to communicate this urgency by organising and intensifying those natural features of language brings poetry into being.

THE GENIAL BUTCHER. I can see that, I can. I have sometimes thought that the market is full of rhythm and rhyme. It is a kind of poetry if you think about it. The life of the market is full of poetry. It isn't poetry that's written down; it's just there, in the atmosphere. That's what I love about the market. It's the poetry. It's the rhythm. Rhythms are everywhere in the social life of the market – the rhythm of commerce, the rhythm of labour. The musical rhythm of the traders shouting their wares. The rhythm of trade, of customer after customer after customer. Rhythms are the music of the market and the music of the city. Rhythm shapes, and is shaped by, the everyday poetry of the market.

THE POET. Yes, it's true. The poetry of everyday life in the market is evident in its rhythm. Language is hopelessly rhythmic because we are ourselves hopelessly rhythmic. We start with the rhythm of the self – the heart and respiration – and attend to the rhythm of the other. Everywhere there is interaction between a place, a time and an expenditure of energy, there is rhythm. What all humankind has known and experienced is potentially available through the poem.

THE DRAMATURG. You still have to do something to capture that, to curate it if you will, to turn the raw material into poetry. Presumably it doesn't just come into being, fully formed.

THE RESEARCHER. But again, that's where you potentially run up against inauthenticity. You have to be careful about the liberties you take with the raw data as you turn it into something else. You have to be careful not to get too far away from the evidence.

THE PROFESSOR. Isn't that what we are doing every time we do what we call analysis? The analytical process surely is precisely the act of turning one thing into another, turning raw data into something meaningful. At its best there is a kind of alchemy at work. The analytical process turns data into something meaningful. As far as I can see, there is no reason why the outcome of that process shouldn't be a poem. Poetry can speak of the meaning of the social world in an intense way.

THE ENTREPRENEUR. Ah, now you're moving on to meaning, and the notion that things are meaningful. The assumption that things mean something is based on the idea that humankind was put on this earth for a purpose, and so there must be some kind of order, some kind of pattern, to human action. It is based on the idea that material objects, practices and events possess immaterial truth and meaning, and that our mission as scholars and artists is to reveal that truth, that meaning. The problem with this is that meaning is not lying around fully formed waiting to be discovered. It has to be made. It has to be generated.

THE RESEARCHER. I don't know. If none of the data mean anything, what is it all for? The intensive labour of negotiation, observation, transcription, annotation, summation, condensation, extraction, abstraction, presentation. The weekly meetings, endless listening to audio files, re-reading transcripts, analysing field notes, annotating interviews, editing videos, reviewing photographs, checking understandings with key participants, discussing data with expert colleagues, scrutinising digital messages, talking with politicians and policy-makers, collaborating with artists and theatre-makers. When all this is done, shouldn't we finally be able to say what the social practice of the market *means*? Isn't that the whole point? Isn't that what we were trained to do? The outcome of the research must mean something. As academic scholars, we have to be confident that we know what to do to recover meaning from transcripts, field notes, digital files, photographs, documents and so on, that we know how to analyse them, and in doing so reveal their meaning. When they have been analysed, their meaning will become available and can be shared with those who have the power to make the world more fit to live in, more equal, more democratic. Isn't that the point? If you lose meaning, you lose everything.

THE PROFESSOR. That's true enough as far as it goes. But remember that all the meaning we ever have is decided by context and consensus. If meaning is discoverable at all in the observable practice of people in and around the market, we do well to avoid the notion that such meaning is fixed and unchanging, or that anything 'means' the same for one person as for another.

THE DOCUMENTARY NOVELIST. I agree that things do not in themselves possess meaning; they have meaning conferred upon them. When we say that something has meaning, actually we give meaning to what we see and hear, touch, and smell, and taste. Meaning is not a simple facet of the interactions between butchers and their customers, or butchers and fishmongers, or butchers and their families.

THE RESEARCHER. During the months we did our ethnographic observations in the market, we were constantly alert to sound, smell, action, interaction, colour, light, atmosphere, language, text and whatever else came our way. We recorded these things as best we could. The meaning of what we recorded is of course in no way fixed, and certainly not certain. But our analysis does allow those meanings to emerge. I have to believe that. Otherwise there has been no sense in any of this. I believe that we should make that process of analysis as visible as possible, so that others can learn from it, and also so that the meaning-making process is transparent and open to question. It concerns me that we might be inclined to background the difficult and creative work of analysis.

THE PROFESSOR. The outcome of the research bears the finger marks of the analyst, in the same way as the sculptor leaves marks in the clay after the piece has been fired. Analysis is always more or less visible, if not always explicit.

THE RESEARCHER. But don't you have to be careful not to take short-cuts, not to merely chop up the voices of the market into so-called poems? Isn't there potential for the analysis not only to be invisible, but to be neglected entirely, to be sacrificed on the altar of the poetic, or the artistic?

THE PROFESSOR. I agree that it is through the hard work of analysis that what we end up with has meaning. But that meaning does not intrinsically live in the butchers' narratives, or in the stories of other stall-holders, or in the traders' signage, or in the fishmongers' shout-outs to attract passing custom, or in the smells of fish and meat, or in messages delivered on WeChat or WhatsApp, or in the ritual interactions of everyday commerce. Meaning is process more than artefact; it is emergent and dynamic, never finalised. Whenever we talk about the market, the meanings change. When we have made presentations about the research in South Africa and South America, Europe and the United States, when we went to the House of Commons to report to the parliamentary committee, when we disseminated our findings to city councillors, when we worked with choreographers, theatre directors, composers, street artists and museum curators, inviting them to creatively respond to, and expand, our observations, when we addressed school teachers and third-sector workers to discuss the social relevance of the research outcomes, when we were invited to speak to religious groups, and to sports organisations, in each of these contexts meaning was differently created, because the audience participants brought their own biographies to bear on the findings of the research. Of course meaning is not unitary. It is not something to be passed from 'us' to 'them' as a neatly packaged whole. Meaning is co-constructed. The histories and experiences of all concerned are directly relevant to this construction of meaning.

THE PRAGMATIC BUTCHER. You went to all those places and talked about our stall? You talked to them in Parliament about our fish balls and pig intestines? About chicken feet and ox hearts? And in America too? Is it true? I would like to have seen that!

THE ENTREPRENEUR

THE DRAMATURG. What I wanted to say was that nothing in the market is really original. That is, everything that is said, or communicated in one way or another, has been said before. Every voice bears the traces of other voices. Everything has in some form or other been said before. Every argument is a response to another argument. Every idea echoes another idea. In that sense there is no such thing as originality.

THE ENTREPRENEUR. That cannot be true. I mean, surely originality is what marks out a work of high quality. It is the difference between the ordinary and the extraordinary. Originality is precisely what I look for in any new piece of work. If you don't have originality, you have no progression. I would go as far as to say that without originality there is no art.

THE DRAMATURG. I am not saying that there is no such thing as an original thought, or an original piece of art. What I mean is that nothing comes from nowhere. The idea that there is some kind of divine intervention that somehow creates an original piece of work out of nothing: that is not the way things are. There is no rabbit to be pulled out of a hat, so to speak. Every discourse is related to another discourse that precedes it, or that runs alongside it. Everything is shaped by something else. What art can do is to make us see the already known in a new light. Therefore nothing is completely original.

THE POET. I can see the sense of that. Markets are a good example. They have been around for thousands of years. They exist in almost any global culture you can name. People trade. They buy and sell. They haggle and they barter, they strike bargains, they compromise, they refuse to compromise, they laugh and joke, they offend, they make comments about each other, they argue, they cooperate, they fight, they swear, they make up, they steal, they share. It has been going on for ever. Markets today go on pretty much as they always have. And they go on here pretty much as they do in other parts of the globe. There are some differences, no doubt, but you won't find much that is original. There may be some differences in technology. But basically buying and selling is buying and selling.

THE ENTREPRENEUR. I can see the argument. But you can't always trace one thing back to another. You can identify patterns, but not always the specific links. And I cannot be persuaded that nothing is original. Surely, even if you are taking a different perspective on, shall we say, markets, you are creating something original, even something new. That is what I call art. It might not be completely different from what has gone before, but it is original. You take what already exists and make it into something new.

THE PHOTOGRAPHER. Yes. I see that. Looking at the familiar with new eyes.

THE PROFESSOR. That is exactly what we tried to do, well, what we did. We collaborated with a group of artists. We asked them to engage with the material we collected in the market, what we called the ethnographic data, the observations, recordings, interviews, all that, and asked them to respond creatively. It was possibly the most exciting thing about the project. We ran workshops over several days with a choreographer, a composer, a theatre director, a film-maker, a street graffiti artist, a museum curator and others. We asked them not only to think about how to engage a wider public with the research outcomes, but also to creatively extend and expand upon the research outcomes. We wanted them to produce something new, something original, from what we already had.

THE ENTREPRENEUR. And so how did that go? What was produced?

THE RESEARCHER. For example, the theatre company we worked with devised a new show in response to the research. They toured it nationally, performing it to audiences twenty-two times in four cities.

THE ENTREPRENEUR. So you made some money on that. Twenty-two performances will have generated reasonable income, as long as your business plan was sound.

THE PROFESSOR. That was not the aim. What we wanted was for people who would not normally engage with the ideas generated in our research to start to think about them. So we did not adopt a commercial model. We wanted new audiences for the research. We took the show to communities who would not normally go to the theatre.

THE ENTREPRENEUR. So what did you make? What was your profit margin? You are not telling me that you took a show out on the road and made a loss?

THE PROFESSOR. It really wasn't about that. It was about raising the consciousness of people who would not normally stop to think about how communication happens in changing urban environments. And it was successful. In the audience reactions, there was a clear sense that people were prompted to think in new ways. In the post-show discussions, audiences were keen to talk about their own experiences of their multi-lingual families. They wanted to talk about multilingual encounters in their own lives. They talked about what we sometimes call translanguaging zones.

THE DRAMATURG. And if I'm right, the performances were normally targeted at audiences in community settings. So they were in day care centres, youth facilities, that kind of thing.

THE ENTREPRENEUR. Oh, so you're saying that these were captive audiences. They were institutional rent-a-crowd shows.

THE PROFESSOR. That is putting it too crudely. And anyway, some of the shows were marketed for the general public and were equally successful.

THE ENTREPRENEUR. But what I am hearing is that they were free, right?

THE PROFESSOR. Yes, we wanted the performances to be available to everyone. So we didn't charge a ticket price.

THE RESEARCHER. I think the theatre work was worth doing. It brought an element of the research to an audience who would not otherwise have engaged with it. But I am not certain that what was eventually produced and performed on stage was closely related to the ethnographic work we had done. There was certainly an attempt to convey something of the multilingualism of contemporary cities. And a multilingual approach in the theatre is unusual enough, original enough if you like, so that was definitely worthwhile. But I found it a bit difficult to discern much of the complexity of communication in the superdiverse city. The ethnographic material did not really find its way on stage.

THE PROFESSOR. But in fairness we asked them to be creative, and to expand on what we offered them. In its own terms, it was a success.

THE ENTREPRENEUR. But not a financial success, from what I can see. Free tickets, community groups. If you are not selling, you are not winning.

THE PROFESSOR. That was never the plan. You can't criticise us for failing to do what we did not set out to do.

THE ENTREPRENEUR. Well, what about the time and effort you put into the collaboration with the other artists? What was it, a composer, a choreographer? That sounds like it has potential.

THE RESEARCHER. The workshops were good. They were creative spaces for collaboration between the research team and a group of committed artists. A lot of ideas came out of that.

THE ENTREPRENEUR. Ideas? Ideas? Can you pay the rent with ideas? Do ideas put bread on the table? What became of these ideas? And if the artists were worth their salt, I'm sure they did not spend several days in workshops for free and gratis.

THE PROFESSOR. Of course, we paid the artists for their time. That is only right. People should not be asked to work for nothing.

THE ENTREPRENEUR. You paid them and they came up with ideas? Is that all?

THE RESEARCHER. That work is ongoing. I have some reservations myself, but it is too harsh to say that we paid them just to come up with ideas. It was about developing a partnership. A collaboration has to start somewhere. It was important to have that time to find out how we could work together. It has great potential. We see it as a starting point. It is easy to be cynical about work with people in the arts, but you have to invest in the long term.

THE ENTREPRENEUR. Oh yes? Well, all I can say is, come back and tell us about the profit margin when you are done. If you are still in the black when the process is over, I will buy champagne for the whole team!

THE PROFESSOR. I still say that profit is not our concern. It would be nice to be able to invest in future partnerships. But that is not our aim. The collaboration with artists is about extending the reach and scope of what we have learned through the research. It is not about turning a buck.

THE PRAGMATIC BUTCHER. But nothing happens without money, does it? I mean, if you want to do more research, the money has to come from somewhere. I'm sure that you have to employ researchers, and they don't come cheap.

THE RESEARCHER. Cheap enough.

THE PRAGMATIC BUTCHER. Wouldn't it be sensible to have a business model that allows you to re-invest, and build on your success?

THE ENTREPRENEUR. There you have it! From the people who know!

THE PROFESSOR. It is not what we do. We are generating knowledge, not making money. We are not in business.

THE ENTREPRENEUR. But the more money you make, the more knowledge you will be able to generate. Is it not so?

THE PROFESSOR. It is just not so simple. I believe in working with artists to bring creative perspectives on research. It offers a new way of looking. We are not trying to turn our observations in the market into a musical by Andrew Lloyd Webber.

THE ENTREPRENEUR. No? Why not? Isn't public engagement with a wider audience exactly what you want? What is the point of the research if it never reaches beyond academic conferences and local community centres? Why not musical theatre?

THE PROFESSOR. All right, in principle there is no reason why not. But the aim is still not to make a profit. It is about knowledge.

THE ENTREPRENEUR. As a wise man once said, first you need to eat. Then you can have your knowledge.

THE PROFESSOR

THE PROFESSOR. You need to hang on to the complexity. Hang on to the complexity of social life by committing to slow scholarship. Making sure you don't lose the richness of the material. What you end up with is an assemblage of ethnographic data, what you might call a polyphonic collage of everyday details. Assemblage is a resource with which to address the heterogeneous within the ephemeral, while preserving some concept of the structural. Assemblage functions as an evocation of emergence and heterogeneity, resisting a finished, finalised state. Assemblage allows the heteroglossia of the everyday to be appreciated. In order for the collage to be assembled, a disciplined, rigorous process of analysis is required, a process of creating and curating what is there.

THE PRAGMATIC BUTCHER. Wait. What?

THE PROFESSOR. What I'm saying, as we said before, is that we create rather than discover meaning. Even when not explicit, the analysis is nevertheless present in the text. Analysis is crucial to the text, as the artist's pencil-made study is essential to the masterpiece – painted over, no longer visible, but always there, a kind of palimpsest. As ethnographic authors, we represent the particular world of the market we have studied, for readers who lack direct acquaintance with it.

THE PHOTOGRAPHER. That is very much the same kind of process I go through with my work. An assemblage of photographs. It is similar to what you are saying. And I agree, such an assemblage, or collage, can never be finished or finalised. It is always changing.

THE PROFESSOR. Yes, I see the resonance, I do see the similarity. It is through the assemblage of material that meanings start to emerge. The concept of emergence offers potential for moving beyond the reification of normative assumptions about social categories. From an emergence perspective, categorisations are reconceptualised as the social positioning of self and other, as positions that are produced through, and emerge in, social interaction, and as always open to change. Social interactions are shaped by the complex interrelationship between the historical and contemporary context of the interlocutors, and the larger societies in which they are embedded. Social categories are sociopolitical emergences that are produced through interactions that are themselves shaped by historical and contemporary processes.

THE PHOTOGRAPHER. But do the meanings emerge, or do we have to do something to the material to generate those meanings? Even if it is only a process of selecting and curating the material? Choosing this image, rejecting that image, does this not make a difference to the meaning of the images themselves? Publishing this field note, rejecting that, and so on.

THE PROFESSOR. Absolutely, yes. You might argue that the raw material itself, the data, as we often say, means nothing much. It has meaning only when we do something to endow it with meaning. Meaning does not emerge unilaterally and unprompted. It must be generated. To generate meaning, we closely examine people's actions and voices where different beliefs, commitments and ideologies come into contact. The contexts in which people communicate are themselves local and emergent, continuously readjusted to the contingencies of action unfolding from one moment to the next. They are also infused with information, resources, trajectories and biographies that can be very different in their reach and duration, as well as in their capacity to bestow or deny privilege and power. Meanings are subject to the contingencies of time and space. The relevance of social action is not finalised but comes into being as we confer meaning on social practice.

THE PHOTOGRAPHER. Don't you think there's a balance to be struck, though, between conferring meaning on artefacts and allowing them to speak for themselves? I agree that we endow objects, voices, stories, photographs, documents, whatever it may be, with meaning, and that is as much about us as about the thing itself. But at the same time, we can let the thing speak for itself. That is how I try think when I am selecting and curating photographs for public exhibition. If they cannot speak for themselves, and stand on their own two feet, they are probably not worth showing.

THE DRAMATURG. There must be a place for informed thought, for intellectual meaning- making. Otherwise, every man in the street is as well equipped to understand the world as the most decorated professor. Surely we are not about to pull down the edifice of the academy entirely?

THE PHOTOGRAPHER. Well, perhaps. But, at the same time, the explanation of the expert should not be overdone. There is nothing worse than an exhibition of photographs in which each image is accompanied by a text which begins 'The meaning of this photograph is…'. The photograph should not need my explanation, my analysis if you like, in order for it to be meaningful, or, if not meaningful, at least ethical. It should be able to speak for itself. The same can be said for paintings, sculptures and any other artefact.

THE ENTREPRENEUR. Is that what it's about, then, not meaning, but ethics? Morals? What about the aesthetic?

THE PHOTOGRAPHER. Yes of course. It's all of the above. The ethical need not rule out the aesthetic, or vice versa. Not by any means. The ethical coexists alongside the aesthetic.

THE DOCUMENTARY NOVELIST. There is the same kind of tension, or the same kind of complementarity, in what I do. I am sometimes told that I should be truer to the people who tell me their stories. But all the voices represented in my books are testifying about a past that is real. I do not make it up. All right, they might not always have said exactly the same words as in the published text, or in precisely the same order as they appear in the text. No one speaks in complete sentences, without pauses or hesitations. I look for what is essential in the narrative. In doing so, I hope that I retain the ethic within the aesthetic. My job is to edit and reconstruct the narrator's words so that what you end up with is more authentic, more true, if you like, than when they spoke.

THE ENTREPRENEUR. Oh good, here we are again with the truth. I thought we had kicked that out twenty minutes ago.

THE GENIAL BUTCHER. I have to say that this all seems to be going round in circles. When are we going to get to the point?

THE PROFESSOR. The point is, or at least the point as far as I can see, is that by observing social practice, whether in a market, or a Polish shop, or a library, or a volleyball club, or wherever people come into contact, by looking really closely and listening carefully, by recording what you see and hear and smell and touch and even taste, and by subjecting those recordings to meticulous analysis, in that way we come to a better understanding of human life. That's it. It's just that.

THE PRAGMATIC BUTCHER. What about if you live that life? Instead of watching someone else living their life, what about living your life? Isn't that a way to come to a better understanding of the human condition?

THE PROFESSOR. Yes of course. The lived experience is the most important thing. In the representation of lived experience, the central idea is expressed not so much through one character or another as through the work's structure. We make meaning from our observations in the market, from service interactions which refer to chicken feet and pig trotters, from WeChat orders for pork and beef from a local restaurant, from complaints about the city council's decision to move the bus stops further away from the market, from narratives about the tough early days of setting up a business. We curate the different voices of the marketplace. But within these voices emerges a cohesion and consistency. All of the voices are included, and are relevant to our understanding of the social practices of the market. All excerpts are analysed, transcripts and translations pored over and annotated, audio-recordings listened to, video-recordings repeatedly watched, online and digital messages scrutinised, photographs examined, discussions held. Analytic memos and summaries are written, commented on and rewritten, vignettes generated and shared across the team.

THE PRAGMATIC BUTCHER. And that is all necessary to understand human life? Really? Isn't a lot of it common sense?

THE PROFESSOR. Yes, maybe it is. But we need to be able to show the evidence. That is the work. That is what we do. If you lose any part of that rigour, you risk losing the validity of what you are doing. It's a process. It is done stage by stage, with quality checks at every point. There are no short-cuts. It is labour intensive. It takes time.

THE PRAGMATIC BUTCHER. And when it's all done, when you have spent all the government money, written all the articles and books, presented to all the international conferences in interesting places, disseminated your key findings to junior ministers in the relevant government departments, collaborated with trapeze artists and tightrope walkers to better engage the sceptical, apathetic public, what then? Is the world a better place? What have you achieved? Is the main outcome anything more than your own pleasure and entertainment? Your own promotion and glittering career?

THE ENTREPRENEUR. Hear, hear! This fellow knows how to ask a question of the esteemed professor!

THE PROFESSOR. It's a good question, one that should be asked, and one that should be answered. It's true that we do enjoy the work. We take pleasure in pushing at the boundaries of the known. That is why we are in the academy. I can tell you, it is not for the money! And yes, we are always aware that we are accountable for spending public funds, and that we have to show very clearly what difference we have made through our research. Your questions are exactly the questions asked of us by the funding body. The answers are not simple, but nor are the questions unfamiliar.

THE RESEARCHER. I do sometimes wonder, myself. I mean, they are fair questions. What difference does it all make? The midnight oil, the bags under the eyes, the financial insecurity, the limited status. What does it buy you? What have you got at the end?

THE DOCUMENTARY NOVELIST. Oh come on, let's not sink into some pit of self-pity. If you want to complain, you ought to live the lives of the people I have interviewed. So many times I have been shocked and frightened by human beings. I have experienced delight and revulsion. I have sometimes wanted to forget what I heard, to return to a time when I lived in ignorance. More than once, however, I have seen the sublime in people, and wanted to cry. I lived in a country where dying was taught to us from childhood. We were taught death. We were told that human beings exist in order to give everything they have, to burn out, to sacrifice themselves. We were taught to love people with weapons. Had I grown up in a different country, I couldn't have travelled this path. Evil is cruel; you have to be inoculated against it. We grew up among executioners and victims. Even if our parents lived in fear and didn't tell us everything – and more often than not they told us nothing – the very air of our life was poisoned. Evil kept a watchful eye on us.

THE PRAGMATIC BUTCHER [to THE PROFESSOR]. So you see – the world is full of suffering. How does your research alleviate the suffering of such people? Watching people buying and selling meat, making notes in your book, writing your articles, collaborating with artists, how does that put an end to the executioners and their victims? How does it clean the air of poison?

THE PROFESSOR. It isn't a fair question. You have to start from the context you are in, begin from where you are. At this point in time and space it is helpful to know how people communicate in superdiverse communities and societies, so that we can improve how we plan the cities of the future. We need as much information as possible, as much knowledge as possible to help us create a future in which people get along together in a convivial way. I believe in that. We have so much to learn. Especially now. It doesn't mean that we are curing cancer or bringing about world peace. We can't do everything ourselves. But what we are doing is worth doing.

THE PRAGMATIC BUTCHER. I'm still not sure that I can join up the dots. But we can let it slide. Is there any more coffee?

THE DRAMATURG

THE PROFESSOR. What we are really grappling with is imitation. We are asking how can art imitate life in a way that allows life to be seen in a new light, and also allows it to be reflected on. And we are also asking how far beyond imitation we can go, or must go, in order to bring life into the light.

THE DRAMATURG. I can go along with that to an extent. But you have to add in politics. It's about bringing life into the spotlight, or footlights, but then saying where are the politics, what difference can art, or theatre, make to the inequalities and prejudices we see around us? In any representation of the social world we must incorporate the political. Working together as a collective, working collectively. That is the way forward.

THE RESEARCHER. I really don't want to be the cynical voice here, but does art really make any difference? Art, theatre, poetry, dance, music, even film, does it make any real difference to the inequalities of the world?

THE DRAMATURG. We can't give up on that. We can't stop believing that there is a role for a theatre of social justice, for emancipatory film, for a poetry of liberation, for radical music. The arts can make a difference to the way people think.

THE GENIAL BUTCHER. I agree. You do see a film now and again that makes you think differently, that makes you want to change the way things are. [To THE PRAGMATIC BUTCHER] What was the name of that film we saw? The one with what's his name, not Beckham.

THE PRAGMATIC BUTCHER. No, Cantona.

THE GENIAL BUTCHER. Cantona. The one with Cantona. That was a good film. Eric. *Looking for Eric.* That kind of thing.

THE DRAMATURG. That's what I mean. An art that represents characters. It makes you think differently. A postman in his everyday life trying to survive. It's not so different from the character of the butcher. In art, we are able to see how people get along, or don't get along. How they joke, tease, laugh, mock, swear, cheat, worry, cry, kiss, wink, shrug. It's all there. The convivial and the everyday. Imitating life and going beyond life, making life anew.

THE GENIAL BUTCHER. And another was that one we got out on DVD. About how he applies for benefits and he dies before he gets it sorted out. That was a terrible story. I cried watching that. There was no way out for him. That was a powerful film. People should see that.

THE RESEARCHER. So it's not just imitation? It's something more.

THE DRAMATURG. I think so. It's imitation which incorporates the critical and the political. I think that's what I mean. It's a process of selection, juxtaposition and commentary, presenting the evidence of ordinary human life in literary form, or dramatic form. Presentation of the material transforms history into a story, blending facts with the literary and dramatic. The stylistic liminality between social practice and literature creates a profound dramatic effect. We are not concerned so much with the particular but with an essence, and for this reason the intention is to capture and represent the emotional history of the experience. Whether it is theatre, or the novel, or curating photography, or ethnography, or poetry, as far as I am concerned the text stands without a main hero. The author feels responsible for multiple heroes, or possibly does not feel responsible for any hero. The author does not accord preferential treatment to any single voice. The author must understand every character and motivate his or her actions. The structural elements of the text are devoted less to the unity of the narrative than to the task of constructing a world of equal voices. The author, binding together plot, style, tone and narrative, is no longer at the forefront. It is no longer the author's story. It is handed over to the characters. It is more about the collective voice. New principles appear for an artistic combination of elements and for the construction of the whole. A belief that there must be more than one way of understanding the world is essential to a new conception of art as collective and critical, and it governs the setting and structure of an artefact. What we are aiming for is to achieve a truly democratic, egalitarian art.

THE DOCUMENTARY NOVELIST. I think that is absolutely right. Every voice is the equal of every other voice.

THE PHOTOGRAPHER. And every image is the equal of every other image.

THE POET. I can see that, I really can. But in celebrating the power of the collective, let's not discount the power of the solitary voice. Don't we also understand others, and understand ourselves, through the lone voice of the poet?

THE GENIAL BUTCHER. It all sounds very utopian. But is it really true? And before you start, I don't mean in the sense of does it represent the truth of the human condition. I mean, is it true that every voice is the equal of every other voice? Is it true that every image is the equal of every other image?

THE PHOTOGRAPHER. It can be, and should be. When I took hundreds, thousands, of photographs of migrants in America in the direst poverty, I represented them alongside each other, without privilege or preference, without commentary or explanation, so viewers and audiences could make up their own minds. Each image stands alongside the next.

THE GENIAL BUTCHER. But some of those pictures became famous, and made you a lot of money, whereas others didn't, so they were not all treated the same. And what about the photographs that ended up on the cutting-room floor? They weren't equal in value to the pictures that made it onto the walls of New York gallery spaces.

THE PHOTOGRAPHER. Well, yes, but that isn't really what I meant. What I wanted to say was that I treated the people in the images equally. It was about the people more than the images of them. It was an attempt at a democratic mode of curation.

THE PRAGMATIC BUTCHER. I don't suppose any of the money you made from the photographs ever found its way into their pockets though.

THE DOCUMENTARY NOVELIST. I think that's a harsh criticism as well. You don't always have that opportunity. You might be sympathetic, but you take the photograph, or you listen to the story, or you record the interaction, and then the moment has gone. You can't support your subjects in any meaningful way, not in the long run. You do what you can. But you would never move on if you felt responsible for the lives of every one of your subjects.

THE DRAMATURG. But if we can't, and if we just use them for our own purposes and discard them, what is the purpose of political art? Aren't we in contravention of everything we believe in? Do we not have a responsibility to our subjects? Are we not in the business of improving their lives just a little? Are we happy just to record their lives, or a moment in their lives, and walk away once we have what we need?

THE PHOTOGRAPHER. The aim is not to support the individual in practical terms, but to raise people's consciousness and make a difference to how they behave in the world, to their beliefs and their actions. One picture, one story, one poem, one ethnography can reach a thousand people, and change the way they see inequality and oppression. Surely that is worth working for.

THE ENTREPRENEUR. But isn't that all kind of hit and miss? You don't really have any clear sense of what the outcome will be. You produce your art and you keep faith that the audience is going to be sufficiently affected, or somehow influenced, to make a difference to what they do in the world. It's all based on a leap of faith. And it isn't always easy to maintain that. It's very hard to be consistent.

THE POET. One of the things about political art is that you have to be very careful about stereotypes. You produce a poem about a racially abused asylum-seeker, a novel about a seventeen-year-old on a zero-hours contract, a film about an un-employed middle-aged man, a play about a crack-addict single mother, a photograph of a woman in an abusive relationship, but do you end up with anything more than a series of stereotypes that your audience has seen before? If not, all they are provoked to do is yawn and scratch their arses, rather than go to the barricades in the name of social justice.

THE DRAMATURG. Well, yes, but stereotypes have their place, don't you think? They enable us to show something of how the world is, and to be critical of the status quo. We say, here, let's have a look at this typical case of, whatever, an unemployed middle-aged man, and let's reflect on why this happens, why there appears to be no way out, what structures in society have created this situation, how can we change it. Stereotypes enable us to stop and reflect on a typification, a typical character. Isn't that what stereotypes are useful for?

THE POET. I can see that. I can see that, but you are still potentially left with an audience that would rather pour a large rum and coke and switch on the TV than engage with politics.

THE GENIAL BUTCHER. Now you're talking.

THE DRAMATURG. Another word we might use is the chronotope.

THE GENIAL BUTCHER. The what tope now? That's a new one!

THE DRAMATURG. The idea that a character is not so much an individual with certain psychological characteristics as the point of intersection of a set of voices in the text. It is the sense that a character is always determined by the particular text in which she or he participates. In this sense, the character is representative of the human condition as it is portrayed in the particular text.

THE POET. I have to say that you have lost me a bit there. Isn't what we need a spark of originality to lift the audience out of its stupor? We have to grab the audience by the collar and make them listen, and make them see. If they are not listening, and if they are not looking, it doesn't matter what we do.

THE DRAMATURG. Well yes. But having said that, it's not that we want the audience to empathise with the characters. We want them to see the action of the market, hear the voices, hold the moment in time while they think critically, while they ask how things came to be the way they are. The characters are not so much people with emotions and feelings, as what I'm calling chronotopes, typical representatives of specific times and places. What I'm trying to say is that we are somewhere between science and art. There's the science of recording the action and speech, the smells and the rhythms, of the market hall. We can recreate what we experienced and make it new for others. That's the science. But the way you curate that science, the way you represent those actions, voices, rhythms and smells, the way you really do make them new, that's the art. We are operating somewhere in the liminal space between the two. Or at least, in a space where art and science overlap. And that is the space where we connect the audience with politics.

THE PRAGMATIC BUTCHER. If you want to stop your audience from yawning and scratching its collective arse, you will have to put your message across more clearly. Not necessarily more simply. But more clearly for sure. Sometimes it is hard to understand what you are all talking about.

THE GENIAL BUTCHER. I don't know. I think he's onto something. Somewhere there has to be a way to change people's minds. There has to be an art, or a science, that makes a difference. Things can't go on as they are.

THE PRAGMATIC BUTCHER

THE PRAGMATIC BUTCHER. I don't know what to tell you. I can tell you that my English sucks. I told you that before. I can tell you that my eldest child is four years old and he corrects my English. I can tell you what it is like to be a migrant in this country. I can tell you how I arrived. I can tell you what it is like to live without legal status. I can tell you about those early years. I can tell you about working as a sous chef in a restaurant, making it up as I went along. I can tell you about the restaurant manager, the way he treated me, despite the fact that he was from my home village. I can tell you about meeting my wife in that restaurant. I can tell you about the long road to earning indefinite leave to remain. I can tell you about quitting the restaurant and moving north. I can tell you about our dreams and aspirations.

I can tell you about memorising the blue book for the citizenship test. I can tell you about taking the test. I can tell you about the person who suggested we go into business in the meat market. I can tell you about the maze of paperwork put in our way by the city council. I can tell you about the traders who stood against our application to open a stall. I can tell you about the man who sold us the business. I can tell you about the real owner of the stall who turned up after the bogus proprietor had run off with our money. I can tell you about the tears we cried when all our savings disappeared. I can tell you about the second time we were cheated and let down. I can tell you how stupid we felt. I can tell you about the times we wished we had never come to this country.

I can tell you about the good fishmonger who helped us write our business plan instead of going home to his family. I can tell you about the day we heard from the city council that our application had been approved. I can tell you about the days and nights we spent fixing up the stall. I can tell you about my first day as a butcher, knowing nothing at all. I can tell you about the money we lost that first week. I can tell you about the learning, the necessary quick learning and the long, slow learning. I can tell you about working out how to cut pork. I can tell you about finding out the hard way how to sell.

I can tell you about when the doctor told us my wife was pregnant for the first time. I can tell you how hard it was when we first tried to find somewhere to live. I can tell you about making that place into a home for the baby. I can tell you what it was like when the baby was born. I can tell you how it was when we got the baby home, and there was just us, feeling proud and helpless. I can tell you about the ups and downs of becoming a butcher. I can tell you about the nights without sleep. I can tell you about the friendships and the hardships. I can tell you about the prejudice. I can tell you about the thefts. I can tell you about the fights. I can tell you about the banter and the laughter. I can tell you about the mickey-taking and teasing. I can tell you about the trust and the mistrust. I can tell you about driving to London on Sundays to pick up boxes of frozen fish balls. I can tell you about carrying buckets of pig blood through the streets.

I can tell you about haggling over prices. I can tell you about the black Silkie chicken. I can tell you about the old man waiting to buy ox hearts every Monday morning. I can tell you about the wholesalers. I can tell you about the woman with cracked skin and broken teeth who comes to change the coins she has earned begging on the streets. I can tell you about the tongue of the ox. I can tell you about goat heads and cow feet. I can tell you about cigarette smuggling. I can tell you about the old Jamaican woman who comes for the chat more than for the meat. I can tell you about the loyal assistant butcher learning a few words of Chinese. I can tell you about rhythm and I can tell you about rhyme. I can tell you about three hundred languages. I can tell you about chicken feet and pig feet. I can tell you about blood, sweat and tears. I can tell you about the flower seller, the nails and beauty man, the shellfish woman, the supplier, the health and safety officer, the woman on the African stall, the shoe and boot trader, the man who does the tee shirts, the Vietnamese woman in the Chinese café. I can tell you about the halal butchers and the exotic fishmongers. I can tell you about the life of the market. But telling you would mean nothing. You have to be there.

PART TWO

Tea

A large mug of strong tea. Salt and pepper pots, a plastic ketchup bottle in the shape of a tomato, chipped blue Formica. Signs on the wall – STEAKS BURGERS COOKED DINNER BEEF POTATO'S GRAVY TAKE-AWAY FISH & CHIPS. A young woman places a bacon sandwich on the table in front of me. The bread is thick and white. The young woman's left arm wears tattoos from shoulder to wrist. The inside of her right arm is inscribed with Chinese characters. Her dyed black hair has been shaved at the back and sides. Outside the window, but inside the market hall, a poster: POULES PLUVERA C'EST DELICIEUX. Hundreds of brightly coloured tins, packets and bottles line the high shelves of REMMISON LTD AFRICAN FOODS. The tattooed woman conducts a loud conversation about her social life with a man in the kitchen. He is frying bacon and wears a heavily stained blue-striped apron. They both have broad local accents. Union Jack bunting hangs from the ceiling in constant celebration. Paint peels from the walls like dead skin.

The pragmatic butcher asks the loyal assistant butcher to pass him a cold drink from the fridge at the back of the stall. You want a can? he asks.
Nah, you're all right, says the loyal assistant butcher.
Don't like Chinese tea, Chinese?
Is it green tea? asks the loyal assistant butcher.
Green tea, not very well, says the pragmatic butcher, making a disapproving face as he swallows a mouthful.
There's a proper Chinese one down the shop, says the loyal assistant butcher.
The proper Chinese tea is not like that, says the pragmatic butcher, that, that is –.
Rose and flowers, says the loyal assistant butcher, completing the pragmatic butcher's complaint.
Rose and flowers, says the pragmatic butcher. In China one kilo about, best one, yeah, ten grand. Ten thousand. Still be one.
Just one kilo? asks the loyal assistant butcher.
Like, like, like a house, if someone wants, higher, higher the price. They do that way so people make money.

THE WOMAN ON THE SHELLFISH STALL. I've been here for fourteen years. The shop's been here a hundred and seventy-five years. It's in the fifth generation now. It's always been family-run. It started with a man called Byron, and it went down. Fifth generation now. Like I say, I've been here fourteen years. I started as a Saturday girl, then a few years later, yes, here I am. Customers-wise, we do still rely on a lot of our old-timers. They've been here, they've been coming for years. But you do get a lot of new customers. Our main trade now is Chinese. They'll come, guaranteed, every week. They probably spend the most money. You have to keep bringing in new lines for them, because it's all fresh stuff, it's all live stuff. The newer stuff you have, they'll try it. Language barrier can be quite a struggle, but I think the more you get to serve them the more you pick it up, really. The same as anything else. We get used to it, we get on with it, we have a laugh, we have a joke. We've got a lad here called Rob and he usually serves a lot of the Chinese, and he's become quite fluent. He knows it all, so usually we just stick him there and let him get on with it. They like him, he likes them. That is the main custom now.

The first time it is a kind of bet with myself, a challenge. It is cold, not yet Christmas, not much going on. The market hall is warm and dry, and the electric lights of the different stalls have a welcoming glow. I stand at one end of the central aisle, the rag market end. I am wearing my black parka with silver fur. I push back the hood. I close my eyes. I stand for at least a minute, listening to the noise. It is first thing after opening, not that busy. I can hear the rhythmic chopping of meat and fish on wooden blocks. The sing-song rhythm of shout-outs of young butchers to attract shoppers to their stall. Running water. Footsteps slowly walking. An announcement on the tannoy tells traders to move their vehicles from the loading bay. Without opening my eyes I take a step forward. It is like stepping onto the edge of a cliff. Another step, and another. Slow, measured, tentative, feeling the ground ahead. Each step makes the sound of the market hall different. Someone honing a knife with a sharpening steel. An electric cutting saw rasping through meat bones. Another step, and another. You all right darling? What you looking for luv? Pork? Chicken? Here you go, all that half price today. Sweetness and spice. Chilli powder. Paprika. Tamarind. Another step. Fish. Herring, or mackerel. Another step. You wouldn't think you could smell kidney, but with your eyes closed you can. That tang of pig's urine. Another step. The polisher on the shoe bar. A key being cut. Another step. Warm smell of leather jackets, handbags, belts, shoes. Another step. Vinegar and salt. Another step. Roasted peanuts. Another step. Sweet and sour sauce. Noodle soup with chicken. Another step. Hiss of steam. Coffee beans grinding. Another step. Air freshener. Another step. Nail lacquer. Another step. Disinfectant. Another step. Turpentine. Another step. Cheese. Cheeses. Savoie. Roquefort. Manchego. Olomoucké syrečky.

watch straps	rat traps
whites booster	feather duster
fly paper	ice scraper
barbeque set	mosquito net
sewing machine oil	aluminium foil
wallpaper paste	turkey baster
sugar soap	towing rope
wasp killer	wine chiller
picture hooks	plaster ducks
fix & grout	insect powder
Elvis clock	sink unblocker
birthday candles	door handles
USB cable	folding table
measuring jug	bath plug
magnetic catch	gate latch
exterior filler	ant killer
reading lamp	workbench clamp

THE HYGIENE OPERATIVE. I mop floors and I clean toilets. I always try to be smartly turned out. It's a public-facing job. You represent the market and you don't want to look too scruffy. So it's clean blue overalls every day, safety boots polished so you can see your face, pressed shirt and tie. Basically I keep the market safe. Officially my job title is Hygiene Operative. But it's more than that. It's health and safety, it's making sure that the environment is at all times safe for shoppers and for traders. On the trolley I carry bin liners, disinfectant, bleach, detergent, broom, dustpan, bucket and a mop. Everything neat and tidy and in its own place. In the top pocket of my overalls I have a ruled Challenge notebook, and three sharpened HB pencils. I make sure every incident is logged and reported, with time, place and the nature of the event. I draw a line under each day. Yesterday a box of cod heads fell from Bartlett's counter and slid across the aisle. Such an incident will leave the floor hazardous. There is the safety of the public to think of, and more and more these days the prospect of litigation. I have three orange fluorescent cones I do put out so people know to keep clear. Last month a live lobster escaped from the shellfish stall. I had to crawl on all fours to confront the creature. It was no joke I can tell you. After a couple of minutes of skirmishing I did manage to grab it. The poor thing must have been scared half to death, claws snapping at the air when I held it aloft. I got a round of applause from some of the shoppers who had seen what was going on. Sheila from the shellfish stall gave me a kiss on the cheek, she was that pleased.

A Chinese woman in her sixties wears shiny purple velvet trousers tucked into purple snow boots, and a purple fur hat. She is accompanied by a purple polka-dot shopping trolley. She stands in front of the pragmatic butcher's stall like a dancer, back straight, heels together, feet slightly turned out. Her eyes are quick, scanning the produce on the counter in front of her. She does not order anything, but mumbles quietly to herself. The woman leaves, shopping trolley lurching uncertainly behind her.

Afghanistan	1p landline	9p mobile
Kenya	1p landline	5p mobile
Mauritius	4p landline	6p mobile
Pakistan	4p landline	4p mobile
Portugal	1p landline	3p mobile
Sri Lanka	3p landline	3p mobile
Turkey	1p landline	5p mobile
Vietnam	3p landline	3p mobile

Out of this world bundles

1000 free minutes unlimited UK texts

THE LOYAL ASSISTANT BUTCHER. I have been working on the stall for eighteen months, working here. Before that I worked on Bennett's, which got closed down. I also worked on Murphy's round the corner. I first started on Enoch's. That's a pork butcher. That's why I came here eighteen months, nearly two years ago; it's easier. With it being coming up to Christmas, I get here about six o'clock in the morning. Plus, we've not got many staff so I'll come in for six. On a quiet day it's half six, but usually six. I come on the bus then get a lift home. I have learned a few Chinese words, like paigu (排骨), niunan (牛腩), laoji (老鸡). When I first started on the stall I was told to remember this word and that word, and all the numbers. So I did. It comes quite easily now. Some of the words I can't pronounce, but when they say it I know what it is. Some of the customers are shocked that I know what they're saying. They think I don't understand. I can do the hand gestures too, for the numbers from one to ten. People are always surprised. But you use whatever it takes. It isn't that hard. Three, four, five, six, seven, eight, nine, ten.

A white-bearded man in a blue and white apron whistles loudly as he walks by. Gentlemen! he says, loudly, and continues without breaking his stride. An announcement over the markets tannoy instructs stall-holders to remove their vehicles from the loading area. The loyal assistant butcher is washing the mirror at the back of the stall. A man in a sleeveless hi-viz jacket leans across the counter to borrow a screwdriver. Don't break it! says the loyal assistant butcher. The man winks and smiles. The pragmatic butcher is sharpening his knives.

REMMISON AFRICAN AND CARIBBEAN FOOD
BARI BARI MUTTON AND GOAT HALAL
BODY PIERCING
SWEET AS CHOCOLATE
C.P. VICKERSTAFFE
MR. FISH
PINOY FOODS
J. BARLOW
ENOCH'S QUALITY PORK BUTCHERS
STREET TALK
HOMECARE DIY HOUSEHOLD
THE BULLRING DELI
XPRESS PHONES
PEARCE'S SHELLFISH
TAK'S CHICKS
CITY TAILORING & ALTERATIONS
ALL SEASONS FISHMONGER
OLIVER'S JEWELLERS
BON CRYSTAL
BISMILLAH BULL RING HALAL MEAT
LEONIE'S CAFÉ
SUNSHINE EAR PIERCING & BEAUTICIAN
SMART SHOES
CHINA MINI MARKET
APRON MAMA CHINESE FAST FOOD
GLOBAL PRODUCE
MEI'S CUISINE
CASH 4 GOLD
BARNES GROCERIES AND FISH

A woman in a headscarf asks the pragmatic butcher for change of a ten-pound note. He finds it for her without complaint. She leaves the market, walking urgently along the sunlit pavement. The loyal assistant butcher bursts into a brief fragment of high-pitched song. He and the Chinese-student butcher are separating pork ribs. The Chinese-student butcher is using the cutting machine at the back of the stall, the loyal assistant butcher wielding an old-fashioned meat cleaver.

THE PRAGMATIC BUTCHER. I woke up at about five twenty this morning and checked my mobile to see if I'd ordered enough stock, or I should put in another order. It was about six fifteen when I arrived at the stall. The suppliers in the wholesale market are here even earlier. Generally I sort out the orders the night before. With some suppliers I have to order one or two days beforehand. They have to order from the slaughterhouse themselves. After the pigs are killed, they have to be hung up for two days before the meat can be cut. Then there's packing and delivery. So it takes time for all the various procedures. There are the hygiene inspections, which happen at the slaughterhouse immediately after the animals are slaughtered. It's different from the way it is in China. It's much safer here, with on the spot inspections. The inspectors spray the meat if they spot anything wrong with it. Any bad meat is destroyed, and isn't allowed to go out of the slaughterhouse. That's why the meat here is much safer than in China. But apparently in China your relationship with the inspector, or your family background, will affect the result of the inspection. It's more a question of who you know than anything. The legal system is not set up in the same way in China as it is here. That makes it difficult to carry out the kind of inspections you find in the UK.

A Chinese man with a large, empty suitcase on wheels is interested in buying pork. He wears a baseball cap with FRANCE inscribed in large white letters across the top. He also wants to buy a kilo of chicken's feet. He is served by the Chinese-student butcher. A new assistant butcher with many tattoos the length of both arms is also on the counter.
One kilo of feet? asks the Chinese-student butcher. The man also buys ribs, and the Chinese-student butcher takes them to the chopping board. Anything else you'd like?
The man shakes his head.
Twenty-three pounds.
The man unzips his suitcase and puts the bags of meat inside.
Throughout this interaction the new assistant butcher with many tattoos has been loudly singing The Beatles' song 'Hey Jude'.

I am gripped with a fear of not being able to deliver on this ethnographic field work. To make things worse, with English as my second language I am anxious about the reality that my field notes will be lined up against those of leading academics in the team who for years have been writing high-quality publications. What if my English is too rubbish to make any sense to them? The benefit of working in a multicultural and multilingual team showed up when I shared my concerns with other team members. It's a relief to hear that the other researchers more or less have similar worries. We talk among ourselves online about these issues and share our stories, tips and advice, to help and encourage each other. It's a shame that we are in four different cities, so that we don't have too much chance to talk to each other face to face. But the academic forums and workshops organised by the project, plus the regular team meetings, do provide a platform to talk about things openly and in depth. My understanding and knowledge of the butchers, and their running of the butcher stall, is increasing on a weekly basis. Conversation with them is getting much easier as we become more acquainted with each other. I had a strong sense of being an intruder on our first day here. We experienced the strong smells of fish and meat (I don't know why as all the produce should be very fresh), the echoing shouts from people working behind the counters, and the banging, clanking and drilling sounds from their tools. We had to stand for several hours a day each time we observed the butcher stall. In order to cause the least interruption to the business we stood beside the cement frames of the huge plate glass windows opposite the stall. It was quite demanding physically. And we were clearly not as unobtrusive as we hoped, as there were many curious stares from all sorts of people in the market – stall holders and their assistants, customers, and even the market police. As time goes by I have noticed that the stares from the nearby stalls are becoming more gentle and friendly. They have started to greet me when I walk past their stalls, and some ask what we are writing in our note books. Some even come over and look to see what we are writing. The feeling of being accepted as part of the market is great, as it enables me to concentrate more on my observation. To build up the relationship with the butchers and win their trust I always treat them with respect and empathy. To me, their entrepreneurship is inspiring, and I always ask them to tell me more about it whenever I have a chance. We share a lot. Especially the two of us women. We are both working mums and immigrants. We often chat about our experiences of moving to the UK, bringing up children, and working here. We talk about the pros and cons of it all. We are gradually becoming good friends. It has become much easier to explain things about the research, and to say what we want the butchers to do. Our relationship is becoming closer as the research goes on.

THE FLOWER SELLER. I'm here five thirty in the morning until six in the evening, Tuesday, Thursday, Friday and Saturday. I sell flowers, and I do plants. Houseplants, garden plants, vegetables. Anything what can be grown or eaten, I sell. A lot of the people who come to the stall don't ever speak to anyone the rest of the week. A lot of them are elderly people. A lot of them are people who aren't working. They haven't got much to talk about. I chat to them and make them feel a little bit better, let them know I'm here. It doesn't matter if people speak to me in English, Chinese, Portuguese. It doesn't make no difference. The market is the heart and soul of the city. People can have a cup of tea, sit down, have a chat. I've learned a few words of Polish, but that's just down to saying thank you. The basics. I can say donkey and I can say bread, but it's no good unless I want to give my donkey sandwiches, you know what I mean?

A waifish young Chinese woman in a long yellow cardigan, red stiletto heels, a red plastic handbag. She buys ribs. The loyal assistant butcher chops them emphatically. The pragmatic butcher serves another customer, chatting at length in Cantonese. The woman in yellow leaves the market hall and totters unsteadily across the road.

THE PORK BUTCHER. I'm sixty-four years of age now, and I came into this market when I was about twenty-three years of age. When I came here I actually couldn't believe the variety of people. The main ones was Chinese, and there was also Filipinos. So this was the new influx at that period in time, if you go back years. I thought, I've been blessed, because I've been to Thailand and places like that, understanding their culture. I thought, yes, I've been blessed, he's put me into the right place at the right time. Of course all their needs are totally different to Mrs Smith and Mrs Jones, chops and sausage and a rasher of bacon; they want the pork, they want it diced up, and livers and tongues, all of the offal, the insides. It was a learning curve for me. You're never too old to learn about this job, because it's an ongoing thing. Over a period of time, then, the Filipinos, they seem to have come to replace the English nurses in hospitals, and all that. Then over the next four or five years, which we're actually experiencing now, all these people from Eastern European countries are coming over, the Romanians, the Polish, the Hungarians, they're coming in. They've got the same eating habits. I don't know if it's a situation where, could I possibly say, like when we had beef in Yorkshire, so they come in, it's a case of chop it up, put it into the melting pot, whatever we've got available, let's have a go for it. It's constantly changing all the time. If it wasn't for the influx of these people, I think the market, generally, would be extremely quiet. There's an income of clientele all the time. I would say your Mrs Jones and Mrs Smiths, it's about two per cent or five per cent of the market, of it all. So it's a blessing, really. I mean, they have no restrictions on pork or that; they come for the belly pork just chopped up, sliced up, and they've got some wonderful dishes with that. That's the Chinese and the Filipinos. The Polish are likewise; they have a little bit of delicacy where they have it smoked, which I don't cater for. They have to go to our neighbours on the deli counter for that, and they're catering for them wonderfully. They have to consider whatever you've got available, either with pork or beef, and they have it all chopped up. Nothing is done like a

Sunday roast scenario. It's just chopped up and put into the pot, served with rice or veg or whatever's available. It's their custom.

SATURDAY STAFF REQUIRED
MUST BE ABLE TO ADD UP!

A large man in a hi-viz yellow jacket gives twenty bags of coin to the butcher. He wears a Bluetooth receiver in his right ear. He smiles, writes in a small booklet, then enters something on his smart phone. The pragmatic butcher takes a leather-bound ledger and writes. He opens the till and starts to empty the bags of coin. The man leaves. The pragmatic butcher brings over to us two cans of cold drink – Tropical Rhythms Mango Carrot. He doesn't say anything, just gestures to shake the bottle, and then a grin and thumbs-up gesture, before going outside for a smoke.

WATER CALTROP
SKY FLAKES CRACKERS
BROWN SUGAR
FORTUNE COOKIES
BEEF FLAVOUR MÌ BÒ
DEMAE RAMEN PORK
PHỞ BÒ
BU ZHI CHUN
DA HONG PAO
GOLDEN MONKEY TEA
YINGDEHONG
LONGJING TEA
SHOUMEI TEA

Cows' feet line glass countertops.
Each hoof, or toe, or toenail, or is it
fingernail, is painted vibrant pink
not carefully, but roughly, clumsily

as if the very last thing to be done
before the sacrifice
was the application
of a small touch of glamour.

A man in a blue shirt and cap brings to the stall three boxes of plastic bags. The pragmatic butcher weighs one of the boxes on the digital scales, opens it and checks its contents thoroughly. Nothing is to be taken on trust.

A fishmonger pulls a delivery trolley, on which are a dozen white polystyrene boxes marked TILAPIA GUTTED AND SCALED. The fishmonger wears a white coat, white cotton peaked cap, blue-striped trousers, white wellington boots. He whistles loudly as he travels.

THE SHOE SELLER. I've been here seventeen years. We've been here from day one, when this market was opened. We were in the old market as well. About seventeen years. The other one was more known. More people knew the other market. Now this one, because of all the change around the market, it's hard to get from that side of Birmingham to this side. The old market was next to the old bus station, and there's no buses around here now. They need to have buses around here to keep this market going. If people can't get here, how the hell are they going to buy? And the car park is very expensive. If you bring your car, it costs you more money. So they need buses for the surrounding area, and the market will be okay. If you're coming by bus then you have to carry your bags. If you've got a long way to walk, it makes it difficult. If you're coming by car, parking is very expensive. To park for one hour is three pounds, or five pounds for three hours. If you're late, that's another thirty-five, forty pound fine at least. They need to sort this out if they want to keep the market going. The city council need to look after it. If they want to keep the market, they need to do something about it. They need to bring people in. Bring them down to our market.

Silkie chicken, very good for your health.
Good for colds, nervous system, immune system.
Good for sickness.
Good for old people.
Good for pregnant women.
Make black chicken soup with garlic, pepper and ginger.

A blonde woman with butterfly tattoos on her shoulder and neck flies through the market. She cradles a young baby in her arms. She is followed by a young child pushing a younger child in a pushchair. The blonde woman presents the baby to one of the fishmongers. He smiles broadly, takes the baby, holds it aloft to admire it, and hands it back to the woman.

STRAWBERRY CORDIAL
ACKEE
FUFU FLOUR
DALGETY HONEY & GINGER
SUPERMALT
CARNATION EVAPORATED MILK
FOSKA OATS
TATE+LYLE GRANULATED SUGAR
COCONUT PEANUTS
FISH TEA
CREAM WHEAT
SMOKED CATFISH FILLET
SMALL IWISA
GRACE SYRUP
GLENRYCK PILCHARDS
NESTLÉ MILO INSTANT MALT CHOCOLATE DRINK
COCONUT OIL
PUMPKIN SOUP MIX
CALLALOO
NIDO MILK POWDER
BUTTER BEANS
MCDOUGALL'S SELF-RAISING FLOUR
BONELESS SALT FISH
ABODI
HONEYCOMB BEEF TRIPE
PLANTAIN CHIPS
GIZZARD
COW FOOT
BIBLE (ENGLISH/YORUBA)

It is drizzling outside. One of those days it never really gets light. The meat supplier with the Bluetooth earpiece speaks to the pragmatic butcher. They scrutinise an order form together. The Bluetooth man is writing in an order book. He is left-handed. He enters something in his mobile phone. The pragmatic butcher counts out a wad of ten-pound notes and hands them to the supplier, who also counts them and folds them, first writing on one of the notes in biro. When business is finished the supplier speaks to the loyal assistant butcher.

Have you got Kay's liver?

Uh? says the loyal assistant butcher.

Kay's liver, repeats the man with the Bluetooth earpiece.

I'll have a look for you, says the loyal assistant butcher.

THE WOMAN ON THE SHELLFISH STALL. A lot of the time we'll ask them what they like and what they eat. It is different to what your average household would eat. Things like razor clams. Everyone eats a mussel or they like crabs, and they like lobsters, but we've got things like sea urchins and things like that, which a lot of people don't know about. If you ask them what they like, and they tell you, we can try and get it. If it sells well we'll stock it. We do a lot of stuff that a lot of other places don't, like we sell live eels. They're hard to get, but we sell loads of them. It's just a case of asking them, really, and working with them to find out what they want, and if we can get it. If it sells well, we'll stock it and we'll always have it. That's what brings them back, because they know we can get it and we can stock it and we'll always have it.

An African-Caribbean woman – tartan wellington boots, close-cropped, yellow-dyed hair, gold half-length parka jacket – bumps into one of the fishmongers. They know each other. She is excited by the unexpected meeting.
Hello, she says, how are you? Long time no see!
The fishmonger responds, you've been busy?
Not really, no. Where are you working now?
The fishmonger points to the fish stall: I'm just here.
They promise to keep in touch.
He returns to his post on the fish counter.
The woman buys half a kilo of chicken's feet from the butcher's stall.

The fishmonger from the neighbouring stall walks past and says to the new assistant butcher with many tattoos in a heavy local accent, you're not having a break already!
Yeahhhhh!, says the new assistant butcher with many tattoos.
They're too nice to ya! says the fishmonger, grinning as he goes on his way.

A little girl with curls and a pink jacket stands alone next to five white plastic shopping bags. Her jacket is inscribed on the back in silver glitter lettering *Betty Fox Dance School*. A very large man, of around twenty-five stone, emerges from the disabled toilet and picks up the bags. He wears the jacket of a suit that has seen better days. The girl follows him out of the market hall to the street.

THE MAN ON THE DELICATESSEN. I've been in the markets thirteen years. Before that I was the area manager of different superstores, working for the Co-op and other leading companies which would frown upon the idea of a market. The market mentality's always meant, I don't mean to sound horrible, but it has meant the lower end of the food trade. We're trying to buck the trend and show it's not, because I know from personal experience that quality in the market is far greater than a lot of quality in the supermarkets. We always aim to keep the quality in what we offer. We're just educating the customers to know that.

A man in a black leather jacket buys a large bag of chicken wings. He has seven other shopping bags, and struggles to carry them. He is one of a group of men of similar appearance, square-jawed, well-built, short back and sides. They each carry large numbers of shopping bags, except one in a grey tracksuit who carries on his shoulder a large sack of potatoes. The men disappear into the rain along Pershore Street.

Shorten legs plain	from £7.00
Shorten legs PTU	from £7.00
Lengthen legs	from £7.00
Narrow legs for seams	from £8.00
Reduce waist and seats	from £7.00
Let out waist and seats	from £7.00
Pockets making hips	from £10.00
Pockets making fabrics	from £10.00
New zip	from £8.00
Lower waist bands all round	from £12.00
Lower bands front or back	from £12.00
Line trousers front or back	from £10.00
Belt loops make and fit	from £8.00
Rubber waist band	from £10.00
Lapped seams by hand	from £8.00
Button holes by hand	from £3.00
Taper fully from hips	from £8.00

THE MAN ON THE CHICKEN STALL. I have been working in the market for the past forty years and I have seen loads of changes. Last week I went to York and I also went to the new market over there in Leicester. It was beautiful, but I just don't see why they are giving money to new markets while they're doing little to keep the old ones. I really can't see why. If you make a place nice, people like to shop there. They love to go there. I went to York and its new market, yeah, beautiful! I spent a thousand pounds there. This market needs investment too. Invest in it and more people will come. This being the second city in the country, it's good for the trade, and it can do well.

A woman in a colourful headscarf and shawl stands in front of the butcher's counter. The pragmatic butcher asks her which pieces of chicken she wants. Hello. The big one? How many? One, two, three? One? Big one? Hahaha, big one! Come on, ten for you, okay? He laughs.
The loyal assistant butcher joins in with the pragmatic butcher's persuasive banter, that one's big!
Too big! says the pragmatic butcher.
The loyal assistant butcher laughs.
The pragmatic butcher goes on with his patter, this one for barbecue, this one better! A little bit fat, over there.
The woman points to one of the pieces of chicken.
That one? says the pragmatic butcher, that one too lean.
How much?' asks the woman.
How much a kilo? Thirty pounds. Twenty pounds. No, no, I am joking. Twenty pounds a kilo, says the pragmatic butcher.
Thirty pounds! The woman throws back her head in disgust.
Nineteen eighty, nineteen eighty, says the pragmatic butcher, quickly.
The woman turns to leave the counter.
Wait, wait, what? says the loyal assistant butcher, you can't, you can't!
The woman pauses, looking back at the loyal assistant butcher over her shoulder, come on! she says impatiently.
Anxious not to lose the sale, the pragmatic butcher offers a new deal. I can do thirty-five for two for you. You want big one? Three hen, four kilo.
How much? says the woman, thirty-five pounds?
Thirty-four, says the loyal assistant butcher, joining the negotiation.
Thirty-six, says the pragmatic butcher, one more pound, three chicken.
Come on, come on, says the loyal assistant butcher.
Be nice, says the woman.
All nice one, says the pragmatic butcher, you want cut cut?
Cut please, she says.

As if from an ancient glacier
it emerges, the head of this young goat
crystals of ice defrosting on eyelashes
and falling as tears.

Suede stubs of horns are not yet full-grown
but surely that implacable gaze
waits only for the final thaw's
long regeneration.

THE MAN ON THE NAILS AND BEAUTY STALL. When we opened it, obviously any business takes about five, six or seven months to get the business up and running, because, two thousand and ten, the end of November, the last owner, he left. So we went to the council, and everyone knows the council takes longer, longer and longer, unless you keep pushing every day, in a crazy way. I did it. Still, for example, the customers were coming in this shop regularly, right? But November two thousand and ten, it just collapsed because the store closed. No customers come. They go. Before that, we'd given all the paperwork to the council. The council took longer and longer. The council should think, our market to build up. They're doing lots of things but sometimes I think they're not thinking very deeply. What it is, November two thousand and ten, the shop is closed now. The one month it was closed, that was the busy time. December, the whole month. They're giving us permission on the twentieth or twenty-first of December two thousand ten, you can open this up on the third of January. We missed Christmas. So everything just collapsed. Then after we opened we would cry every day, how are we going to pay the rent? This and that. Then, again, the council helped us, half rent, this and that. Then you build up, okay, full rent after two months or three months. Whatever is there, it's okay. Now, the council shouldn't put it up, but they did it. It's okay. What can we do? You know, they process them. I'm giving the city council a paper, and I'm giving them the same paper, after a few days. She's giving the same paper after a week, maybe, still on the desk, the paper is there. It's not one-handed, it's not fair, if I say okay, straight dealing is a different thing, but the city council is irritating. It's a different system. Anyway, after seven or eight months the business was okay. Two thousand and eleven good, two thousand and twelve we dropped about five per cent in business, two thousand and thirteen dropped about ten per cent down, the same two thousand and fourteen. At the moment, you can see, it's really quiet.

The supplier with the Bluetooth earpiece stands in the entrance to the stall. The pragmatic butcher counts out twenty-pound notes for him, but the supplier has clearly lost count and shakes his head. The pragmatic butcher laughs and makes a drinking gesture with his hand. Too many drinks! he says. The supplier smiles. The pragmatic butcher writes in his notebook, and the Bluetooth man keeps a record in his own. Okay, I'm gonna crack on, says the supplier. Thank you very much, he says, see you in the morning.

An altercation at the disabled toilet. Two of the cleaning staff are telling a group of older people that the regular toilet is round the corner. This toilet is only for disabled people. It ends in jokes and smiles.

THE WOMAN ON THE AFRICAN FOOD STALL. I have been working in this market for seven years. I sell only African food. I came from Nigeria and most of my stock has to be imported. At the moment business is slow, like everything else in the market. Lots of people are out of jobs, and people don't have much money to buy things they can do without. The management here is the worst. Everything is too expensive, the rent and rates. The market doesn't do much to help us. And the meetings with the city council don't help at all, although we are constantly meeting up with them, the committee and everything. But they are not willing to reduce the rent, and that affects the business.

The pragmatic butcher is on his mobile phone. He places a blue carbon copy sheet beneath the page of his order book. He checks the calendar on the wall, writes in the order book, and checks the calendar again.

THE GOOD FISHMONGER. When my uncle first came to this country from Pakistan he didn't speak any English at all. He got his friends to help him and, you know, he clucked like a chicken when he wanted to buy chicken in the market. Ha ha! Tuck-tuck! Sounds like a chicken! *The fishmonger performs a dance which mimics the actions of a chicken, his foot scraping the ground, head bobbing forward and back.*

Curry Chicken Fried Rice £5   Chicken Fried Rice £4.50
Curry King Prawn Fried Rice £6   King Prawn Fried Rice £5.50
Curry Beef Fried Rice £6   Special Beef Fried Rice £5.50
Curry Potato Rice £4

THE PORK BUTCHER. The downside is they come over here and it's inbred where they've got to haggle. The Romanians are the worst ones. I don't know if it's because they're gypsies or it's their culture, and everybody wants to haggle, but they take it to the far extreme. Sometimes it can be tiresome. Extremely tiresome. Nothing is a straight sale any more, in the sense of, I want to spend ten pounds, yes, that comes to twelve pounds. I'll give you an example. A piece of pork, twelve pound sixty. Twelve pound, all right? No. I need the sixty pence. Sixty pence? What's the matter? It's only sixty pence. I say, sixty pence is twelve shillings. I've worked all day for that many years ago. You're heading towards seventy-five, which is fifteen shillings. I worked for a week for that when I was part time. That's over their head. That's a waste of time.

I only say those kinds of things when I'm extremely tired. You have to put up with it, you say, that's a fair price for the margin I have, you've got quality at a fair price and we chop it up.

An elderly man walks by, holding the hand of a small child.
What's that? asks the child.
They're chickens, says the man, without pausing or interrupting the rhythm of his stride.

THE SHOE SELLER. I've been in this country fifty-six years. Some of the new immigrants call me an immigrant. I'm older than their grandparents. Before the Asians, there used to be Welsh, English and Scottish. They were immigrants too. They came to work in the Midlands, like we came through later. My parents came later. All the Welsh miners used to come and work in the Black Country on the smelting, in the foundries.

Bare pig carcasses piled high on a metal trolley.
Twenty or more of them complete
but for the head and internal organs.

On the next trolley in line more carcasses
hung from the feet, tails intact
the biggest of them almost as big as bulls.

THE MAN ON THE NAILS AND BEAUTY STALL. When the bus route was there, just there, outside there, all the customers got off straight into the market. That was a benefit for old people especially. They were just trolley, get off, do the market. Going just outside there, jump in the bus going home. The bus route, since it closed from here, trust me, it's a very down business. Very down. Secondly, just because this New Street Station is making, is redeveloping, New Street Station, now, they move to the other site. When New Street was here, the train station I mean, people think, coming from Manchester, Scotland, various places, they don't know Birmingham well. So when they have something to buy or to do threading or anything in our business, they think, I've got half an hour's time, let me pop round. When they pop round, people say, go in the market, there is a threading shop, there are other shops. Or if you want to buy, you can buy from there, it's huge, a good discount, blah blah. Lots of people, they used to come, and whenever they'd come they'd say, sorry, my train is in about ten minutes' time, can I have this done? Yes, you can have it done. My train is in ten minutes, can I have this? But now it's sorry, so sorry. Whatever is there, the bus stop's moved, New Street Station has moved. Just because of that, as far as I know, the market has collapsed. No matter how many advertisements they do, I don't think they will make up for that.

PUKKA MEAT PIE'S £1.50 EACH 4 FOR £5
5 KG PORK SCRATCHINGS NOW £22.00
HAND RAISED PORK PIE SMALL £1 EACH
ONION BAJI 99p EACH
BRAWN 99p FOR 100 GRAMS
£3 EACH HONEY ROAST HAMS
AWARD WINNING POLONEY
BLACK PUDDING 50P TODAY ONLY
£15 EACH GALA AND ASCOT PORK PIES
2 FOR A POUND ASSORTED SLICES
£1 BEEF DRIPPING
AWARD WINNING WHITE PUDDING
SMOKED HAMS £40 ONLY TODAY
BOILING JOINT TOP QUALITY £5 ANY TRAY
PURE LARD 2 FOR £1.00
PRESSED HODGE ONLY £1.00

A young African woman stands in front of the butcher's stall. The butcher slowly puts on a pair of heavy black rubber gauntlets while waiting for her to speak. He says nothing to her, and she moves on without speaking.

BREAKING BAD
MACHINE HEAD
WALKING DEAD
MOTORHEAD
LYNYRD SKYNYRD
MARILYN MANSON
HARLEY DAVIDSON
IRON MAIDEN
SYSTEM OF A DOWN
THE BOYS ARE BACK IN TOWN
UNDERSTANDING AMERICA
METALLICA

NIRVANA
SONS OF ANARCHY
AC/DC
NEVER MIND THE BOLLOCKS
LOS POLLOS HERMANOS
SLIPKNOT
DAVID BOWIE
THIN LIZZY
BOB MARLEY
AVENGED SEVENFOLD
BUFFALO SOLDIER
GUNS N' ROSES
QUIET RIOT
BLACK VEIL BRIDES
SABBATH BLOODY SABBATH
MEGADETH

Inside a tiny prefabricated room stands a hospital-style bed, or trolley, its cream-painted metal frame capable of ascending and descending, and of raising the patient into a seated upright position. A small control box with two buttons is attached to the wall next to the hospital trolley. A ringleted cable connects the control box to the patient. The trolley has four small wheels, which are lockable. A rubber mattress is covered with a polyester sheet in leopard-skin print. Beside the trolley is a cream-coloured plastic storage unit with three drawers. This too is on four small wheels. On top of the storage unit, on a sheet of cream-coloured muslin, stands a white plastic pot, or container of some sort, with a lid. Beside the container are two bottles of hand cleanser, or steriliser, one white, the other green. The white bottle is almost empty. Beside the storage unit stands an electric radiator. In the corner of the room, wedged against a light switch, a bunch of wooden roses, or they could be tulips, orange and yellow. On the cream-coloured wall, stuck with Blu-Tack, several laminated photographs. One displays the serene face of a man, a piece of silver metal in the shape of a horseshoe through both of his nostrils. A disembodied navel, probably a woman's, is adorned with a paste diamond, and a trailing string of silver stars. A lower lip wears blue pearl-sized spheres at each end of a long, narrow stud. An earlobe is decorated with a cylinder of bronze, half an inch in diameter and an inch long. A woman's face stares into the middle distance, bearing a dozen or more studs, rings and other metal piercings. Another woman looks into the camera, heavy with mascara, most of her face covered with a silk crimson scarf. A single silver stud disappears under her left eyebrow, and resurfaces above.

THE MAN ON THE MENSWEAR STALL. I've worked here the last nine years, and we sell menswear, exclusive menswear with jeans, trousers, combat, rock gear, rock tee shirts, all kinds of stuff we sell. The customers, we get all different types of customers. Asian, Chinese, West Indians, English, all different types of customers we have. The customers, most of them, are very good. We have some regular customers. Very often we get passing customers as well. We're only suffering since the bus stops have been changed. We're suffering from that because we're not getting all the people that used to come in the market. We're not getting those people any more now. That's the main effect on the market. Otherwise we're just surviving. The footfall is down now due to the change of the buses, and the parking is very expensive in the city centre. Parking is very expensive. The bus fare is more cheap these days, but all the routes have been changed. So that's really affected the market as well. That's not only me, that's all the other traders. Even specialist butchers. They're struggling as well.

The pragmatic butcher sits cross-legged on the windowsill. He eats his lunch from a Tupperware box. It is left-over pork dumplings from last night's dinner. He eats silently and with enthusiasm. An ambulance hurries by with blue lights flashing.

Warning
Please do not talk when the machine is on.
当电锯开动时,
请勿和他说话,
以免意外发生。

康記肉舖

天天新鮮運到
我們提供新鮮豬牛肉
豬紅,豬肚,豬肝,豬腰,粉腸
生腸,豬橫利等。
新鮮豬牛肉
(豬扒,豬腩肉,豬頸肉,
豬肘,牛腩)
福建小吃(福州魚丸)

新鮮 豬牛羊 歡迎批發

Blood

The genial butcher and the pragmatic butcher carry pig blood from the slaughter-house in galvanised metal buckets. If the market lift isn't working they go through the shopping centre. Sometimes the blood spills on the floor and they have to clean it up before the security officer catches them. At first, when they try to make blood curd they don't understand why the blood won't coagulate. They discover that you can't mix the blood from different pigs in the same bucket. They pour away several buckets before they work it out. After several attempts they realise that you have to add water and salt. You don't boil the blood. It thickens and becomes solid on its own. If you don't add water it is too hard, but if you add too much it becomes viscous. And you need the right measure of salt to taste. The couple used to get the blood for free, but not anymore. Back then it was pure profit from blood curd.

The researcher sets up the pragmatic butcher and the loyal assistant butcher with digital voice recorders and tie-clip microphones. There are smiles all round.
It's BBC One recording, hahaha!! says the pragmatic butcher.
The loyal assistant butcher laughs.
The pragmatic butcher says to the researcher, in Mandarin, do you have a brush to lend him, so he can have a prettier hairstyle? Hahaha!!
The loyal assistant butcher has too little hair to require brushing.
The researcher tells the loyal assistant butcher, he says you can brush your hair so you look pretty!
The loyal assistant butcher laughs, and strokes his bald pate.

THE YOUNG FISHMONGER. I graduated from the Birmingham College of Food and Tourism. I started working in the market when I was eighteen and I have done loads of trades like jewellery, catering, fish, meat and everything. A lot of my customers come from Manchester, Leicester, Walsall, Wolverhampton and so on. For me, working in the market is about making customers happy, making friends with them and the people working around you. You have got to improvise for your business. And we have customers who are Romanians, Polish, Czech, Bulgarian and Hungarian, and many more. They don't speak much English. That's not a problem. They can write things down for us. And we have people working in the market who can speak Polish, or Romanian, or Czech, and they can help us with it. Romanian, Polish and Czech, they are all different but somehow they are similar to each other, so if you can speak one of them you can figure out the meanings of the others more or less. And you can use your body language as well. If you slouch, and stand here with a long face, no one wants to shop with you. So I always stand straight with a smile on my face, always ready to serve.

THE LONG-SERVING BUTCHER. I've been in the market now thirty years. I've been working for the same firm for twenty-seven years. Culture-wise, it's changed in that time. More foreigners now that we're serving. Kosovans, Albanians, they're the more pork spenders. Some of the customers don't speak much English, so they point. They just point, or if not, I served two last week, couldn't speak a word of English, and I got them in the fridge, they showed me what they want, I took eighty pounds off them straightaway. It was good. They just point. You try to entice them in, show them, ask them what they want, and then they do it. They come to the market because it's all here, nice and fresh for them. People always want a market. They buy a hell of a lot of pork. They don't eat lamb. They'll eat beef as well, but they won't eat lamb at all. They just like pork. They will spend anything from sixty pounds to three hundred pounds. That's one family, honestly, absolutely amazing. I remember last Christmas, three Kosovans came and we took fourteen hundred pounds off three of them. Three of them together, fourteen hundred pounds. Just to be ready for Christmas and New Year. Absolutely unbelievable.

THE GENIAL BUTCHER. We keep the prices low to attract customers. When people cook at home, whether they choose to buy more or less, it is good for business. Buying meat is a daily necessity for most households, but you only go out for dinner when you have extra money to spare. We used to sell hens at seven pounds for three, but we could only sell three boxes a day. Now we have lowered the price to six pounds for three, and we can sell ten boxes a day. So now we can compete with our rivals. It's good for our relationship with the suppliers as well. It makes it easier to bargain over prices when we're making bulk purchases.

THE MAN ON THE DELICATESSEN. This stall started off as an old-fashioned English delicatessen, but obviously as time has moved on, with the amount of different nationalities, we've diversified into doing as much range as we can, basically to fill the need of every nationality coming into the city. We are generally still an old-fashioned delicatessen, which is just not seen around, especially not in the city centre, because there's not the call out there. Although we do very well at what we do. There's not many of us still left, unfortunately. Luckily a lot of our visitors to the country understand more on the delicatessen lines than the English people. We're capitalising on that, and benefiting from them.

Freshly delivered every single day
We supply fresh pork and beef
Blood curd
Pig stomach
Pig liver
Pig kidney
Pig intestine
Pork belly
Fresh pork and beef
Pork steak
Pork belly and neck
Beef steak
Beef joint

Nǐ hǎo! Two men stop by the butcher's stall. They are not Chinese.
Nǐ hǎo! The pragmatic butcher mimics the first customer's exaggerated Chinese accent.
The man repeats his greeting, nǐ hǎo!
The genial butcher says nǐ hǎo! back to him, without her husband's mimicry of the man's exaggerated, mocking inflection.
The customer chooses fillets of pork. The genial butcher chops them into small pieces for him.

The butcher stands at his wooden chopping-board
in a red and white striped apron.
He takes up his sharpest knife and trims the hairs from a pig's trotter.

He studies each individual hair before removing it.
He could hardly be more assiduous
if he were a high street barber giving his best customer a Turkish shave.

There are two trolleys full of deliveries, which the three men begin to unload. The loyal assistant butcher starts to move the boxes of meat and offal one after the other, passing them to the Chinese-student butcher, who is standing in the middle to take the boxes from him. He in turn passes them to the pragmatic butcher in the storeroom. The pragmatic butcher lays the heavy boxes on top of each other on the floor beside the door. There is hardly enough room in the store for the new stock.

ERE Y'ARE DARLIN
ERE Y'ARE
ALL THAT FOR TEN POUND
THAT WHOLE TRAY FOR TEN POUND
ALL THAT CHICKEN HALF PRICE TODAY
TRAY OF CHICKEN HALF PRICE TODAY
WHEN IT'S GONE IT'S GONE
BUY ONE GET A FREE ONE
TEN POUND YOUR CHICKEN THIGHS
TEN POUND DRUMSTICKS AND THIGHS
A WHOLE TRAY ONLY A TENNER
GET THE MOST FROM YOUR TENNER
THAT WHOLE TRAY ONLY TEN POUND
COME ON DARLIN HOW DOES THAT SOUND?
THAT TRAY HALF PRICE TODAY
ALL THAT HALF PRICE TODAY
ONLY TODAY DARLIN
COME ON DARLIN
YOU WON'T DO BETTER THAN THAT
YOU WON'T FIND CHEAPER THAN THAT
TEN POUND A TRAY YOUR CHICKEN
TEN POUND A TRAY YOUR CHICKEN
TEN POUND A TRAY
TEN POUND A TRAY
HALF PRICE TODAY
HALF PRICE TODAY

THE PRAGMATIC BUTCHER. I came here in 2001. I had relatives in the UK. I met my wife in 2006, when we were working in Kent. Her sister was working there, so that's where she went to start with. Neither of us had worked in catering in China, but we met in a take-away restaurant in this country. I knew how to eat with chopsticks, that's about it. I knew nothing at all about cooking. They took me on as a sous chef. My second year here I almost went home. I had such a bad foot injury. It was so painful. I really wanted to go back home. I didn't have it before I came to the UK. Number one, I think the problem was that I had to stand all day long in my work. Number two, I was so stressed. It was very painful. I didn't learn that much English when I was in China, but I really wanted to go out and see the big, wide world. You get inspiration from the people in your village. They go abroad, and send money back to their families, who can then afford extravagant houses and a good life. Of course, those who have gone abroad don't tell their parents or families about the hard lives they have had overseas. So when you hear their stories you want to follow in their footsteps.

An elderly woman, African-Caribbean, tall, well-dressed.
Is your grand-daughter off school this week? asks the loyal assistant butcher.
Yeah, she's in Croydon today, says the tall woman. She's off this week; the children are not there so she is not teaching, but she's still in school a lot. Too much work to do!
The loyal assistant butcher comes out from behind the counter, opens the lid of the woman's shopping trolley and slips her meat carefully inside. He securely buckles up the trolley for the woman.
See you next week then, she says as she walks away, pulling the trolley after her.
You will, says the loyal assistant butcher. He stands and watches as she leaves.

A Chinese woman buys pork at the counter, where she is served by the Chinese-student butcher.
六镑三 says the Chinese-student butcher, telling the woman the price.
六镑三. The new assistant butcher with many tattoos is also at the stall, and loudly mimics the Chinese-student butcher, looking at the woman to see her reaction. The woman is unimpressed by his attempt to show off his language skills. She turns away from the counter without looking at him.

The pragmatic butcher's mobile phone rings. Hello, he says. You want the ones with bones. Ask him to order in one go. Ask him to order all together. All at the same time. Okay, okay, ten kilos, no problem. Okay, bye.
He ends the call, and says, fucking Pepper!
Who is it? asks the loyal assistant butcher.
Pepper! Kidney, they wanted it yesterday already!
How much, how much is it? asks the loyal assistant butcher.
Ten kilo, says the pragmatic butcher.
Ten kilo?
Oh, shit! says the pragmatic butcher. He has cut his hand with a knife.
Careful, says the loyal assistant butcher, health and safety.

THE GENIAL BUTCHER. We had worked in restaurants, but neither of us had worked in butchery before. We didn't even know how to cut meat. At six o'clock on the first morning my husband went to the wholesaler and asked how much stock he needed. The wholesaler said he would need at least seven hundred pounds' worth for the day. So he bought seven hundred pounds' worth of meat and offal. We hadn't got a single customer yet. Nor did he have a car, so he piled the meat into a supermarket trolley and pushed it down the street to the market hall. When he was back at the stall he dumped the stock on the counter. He just stood and looked at it. He phoned me at home, and told me we were completely stuffed. By the end of the week almost all of the meat was still there. We had to sell it off at huge discount. We lost money with each sale. The next week we decided for ourselves how much stock we needed. We worked so hard to learn how to cut whole pigs and sides of beef into pieces of meat we would be able to sell.

The price tag says 老鸡, translated literally as old hen. This is to do with the traditional Chinese recipe for making chicken soup by using aged hen meat. It is said to be the most nutritious kind of meat. It is particularly beneficial to the weak and sick, people recovering from an operation, and women who have recently given birth.

THE GENIAL BUTCHER. One of the butchers really bullied us when we first started. My husband eventually had a fight with him on the floor of the market hall. It was a really bad fight, involving meat cleavers. There was blood all over the place. It could have been really terrible if the other traders hadn't intervened to stop it. It happened not long after we set up our stall. Some of the other traders were such bullies.

THE MAN ON THE NAILS AND BEAUTY STALL. When we opened we used to pay twelve thousand five hundred pounds. No, twelve fifty rent a month, we used to pay. Now in two thousand and twelve, vroom, it went up, the high rates. It was three hundred and fifty extra, so we were paying six hundred. No, sixteen hundred, sorry. One thousand five hundred and eighty-two pounds and three pence. I could show you the bills. If it is the previous rate and rent, we would be happy. At the moment, the one side is that the market is going down and the rent has gone up. You can imagine, how will we pay the rent? Not for us, for everybody. In the meantime, two thousand and twelve and two thousand and thirteen, lots of stalls were closed. Now, where will people go? Lots of people are jobless and this and that, so everybody has to pinch their pennies for living life, to keep their stomachs full. Some of the stalls now are slowly, slowly picking up. December time, maybe it will start in two weeks' time maximum, the German market. The German market starts at the other side of the city. If the

German market starts at that end to that church end, yes, half of it, yes, we could make a few pennies from here, but the German market isn't even here. It's the other side of the city centre. Somehow, obviously we are here, why? Because we can pay rent somehow. Instead of two breads we're eating one bread, but we're paying rent first, because we have to carry on the business. It's good and bad, and it's hard.

What's the difference between the yellow ones and the white ones? A thick-set man in a sheepskin coat points to two piles of chicken drumsticks in different trays.

I can sell twenty cases of the yellow drumsticks in a day, but only one case of the white, says the pragmatic butcher. You tell me the difference.

I'll have two kilos of yellow and one kilo of white. The customer taps the counter glass with a nicotine-stained, stubby forefinger as he speaks.

The pragmatic butcher scoops the chicken into plastic bags.

The man taps the glass again. I said one kilo of each! He raises his voice and stares at the pragmatic butcher.

The pragmatic butcher looks squarely back at the man. You said two kilos yellow, one kilo white.

Okay, so I changed my mind. The customer is not smiling.

The pragmatic butcher weighs the chicken in two separate bags. Eleven pounds all together. He ties up the bags and places them on the counter.

Nine pounds, says the man, offering a ten-pound note. The customer holds out his other hand, demanding change.

Ten pounds, says the pragmatic butcher. He takes the note and slips it into the till.

The man stands with his hand still extended, unwavering in his gaze.

The pragmatic butcher folds his arms.

The white clock in the high corner of Enoch's quality pork stall is marked with numbers written in Chinese characters. 十二 means twelve, 九 means nine, 六 means six and 三 means three. The stall's name is translated into Chinese characters: 以诺士

THE MAN ON THE DELICATESSEN. We're losing a lot of the older customers. Obviously we've got a lot of the newer, younger customers who are coming in; a lot of the time they're looking at different recipes, the different cookery programmes that are coming on. They're experimenting more, whereas years ago people used to basically eat their meat and vegetables and that was it. Now we're getting a diverse amount of people coming in, which is good for us. It means we have to keep moving with the times. A lot of the problem is with the delicatessen, because we've actually lost our way with the delicatessen. When they see 'delicatessen', the word 'delicatessen' has been used by a lot of the coffee companies. So a lot of the coffee outfits call themselves a delicatessen. They're not. They're serving coffee and cake, which I find a bit insulting after all the years of training to get into the delicatessen game, to find out some coffee shop chains have classed themselves as a delicatessen because they're serving a few cakes. Then again, it's just re-evaluating what we're doing, and getting people back into it, and used to it.

The pragmatic butcher goes out for a smoke and stops to chat to a group of men gathered at the market entrance. Among them are two fishmongers and several other traders who work at stalls in the market. The pragmatic butcher speaks loudly to a short, African-Caribbean man dressed in a dark suit and a bowler hat, who seems to be the centre of the group's attention. Who are you? he says, I don't recognise you! The crowd explodes with laughter. The short man in the bowler hat laughs as well. All the others in the group are in white uniforms and greasy, full-length aprons.

THE GENIAL BUTCHER. This isn't our first attempt to set up a business. We tried quite a few times, even when we didn't have legal status to stay in the UK. We were conned the first time we tried to set up a business. It was our first attempt, and the business was taken away only two weeks after we set it up. We were conned by a man from Fujian. I trusted him because he was from the same place as me. But he knew we didn't have legal status and he took advantage of our eagerness to start up a business. We paid him five thousand pounds in cash for a take-away restaurant, but it was only open for one day before the real owner of the property rang asking us what we were doing in his place. The man from Fujian sold us the business, but it turned out he didn't even own it. The restaurant was leased to him by the real landlord. We had spent almost two weeks cleaning and polishing everything, but we had to leave as soon as we were open. The man we paid money to was nowhere to be found. He ran away with our savings. Soon after that the owner closed it down because the man hadn't paid his rent. We were conned out of the five thousand pounds. We couldn't sue him because we didn't have legal status. We had nothing left, and we had to work in separate take-aways again, to provide for ourselves. After saving up for more than a year we tried again, but we were conned again. This time we didn't lose money but we were let down by people who cheated us. By this time we didn't know who to trust. We had to live in different cities just to make a living. I got pregnant in two thousand and nine and moved to Birmingham because the rent was much cheaper than it was in London. My husband worked in London for about a year, then moved to Birmingham to join me. After we got legal status we thought about trying again to set up a business. The person I shared a house with said why not open up a stall in the market? So we decided to give it a go. Some of the stall holders were really horrible. I think it's because we are Chinese. But here we are. To be honest, there were also some really nice people who helped us. You know, one of the fishmongers next door, the younger one, he taught us how to write a business proposal. It was him suggested we see the boss of the market. He told us some of the other traders were against us opening the stall, but he managed to find others who supported us. So he started a campaign for us outside the market among the traders who were supportive of us opening the business. And we started it like that. And now we tell our customers that we are the first and only Chinese butcher in the city!

The pragmatic butcher finishes unpacking the day's delivery, and begins to put different goods for display in the trays underneath the glass counter. He holds a box of pig blood curd. He delicately takes out one piece after another, lining them up in one of the aluminium trays.

How much a kilo of that? A young man in a black tracksuit and backwards-facing baseball cap jumps onto the concrete step in front of the counter and points at a tray of beef.

How much you want? More cheap! says the pragmatic butcher.

Nǐ hǎo! The customer greets the pragmatic butcher and, pleased with his intervention, turns to the Chinese customers around him, loudly repeating, nǐ hǎo! nǐ hǎo! in a faux Chinese accent. Everyone ignores him. The pragmatic butcher, however, engages with his customer. Twenty pounds a kilo, and more cheap.

Six kilos, says the man in the baseball cap.

Sixty kilos? Right! The pragmatic butcher jokes.

No, no, six kilos, says the man, impatiently.

Sixty kilos! Six zero kilos? The pragmatic butcher persists with the joke.

Oh, hehehe, how much if it's sixty kilos then? asks the customer, humouring the pragmatic butcher.

The pragmatic butcher laughs but does not answer.

The man orders chicken wings, chicken breasts and pork bellies. How much altogether?

Forty-seven, says the loyal assistant butcher, who has been watching, and keeping tabs on the prices.

Forty-five, says the customer.

Forty-six, says the loyal assistant butcher.

The young man hands over five ten-pound notes. The loyal assistant butcher laughs and says, should I keep the change for next time? We've given you too much discount. The man laughs too. He takes his change and the bags of meat. He shouts to a man who is waiting for him beside the windowsill. The second man picks up two of the bags and they leave the market.

꙱

BEEF BELLY £2.70/LB
BEEF SHIN £6.20/KG
OXTAIL FROM £5.00/LB   £10.29/KG
OX TONGUE £2.26/LB   £4.99/KG
BEEF FLAT RIBS £4 FOR 9 KG
BIG PIG FEET £1 EACH
SMALL PIG FEET 3 FOR £2.50
PIG'S TAILS £2.69/KG   2 KG FOR £5
PORK SHOULDER 2 FOR £5 OR £3 EACH
PORK RIBS £2.26/LB   £4.99/KG
RUMP STEAK £7.99/KILO
CHICKEN FEET £1.13/LB   £2.50/KG
DRUMSTICKS £2.50/KILO
CHICKEN WINGS £1.13/LB   £2.50/KG
CHICKEN THIGHS £1.15/LB   £2.50/KG
FAT END & UTERUS £4.99/KG
PIG'S KIDNEY & LIVER £2.50/KG
PIG'S TONGUE £1 EACH 3 FOR £2.50
SNOUT £1.49
LUNG £2.50/KG
KNUCKLES £1.50/KG
MASK £1/KG
BLOOD CURD 60P/KG
COW EARS 50P EACH
PIG'S HEART 60P EACH 2 FOR £1
BEEF HONEYCOMB £3.99/KG

The pragmatic butcher and the loyal assistant butcher discuss the purchase of a new chopping block for the stall.

Six fifty for the new block, says the loyal assistant butcher.

Six hundred? asks the pragmatic butcher.

And fifty, says his assistant.

No, small, small one.

That was five hundred.

Pound? asks the pragmatic butcher.

Pound. Three foot by two foot, seven inch thick, six fifty.

Yeah, that one, very normal one, says the pragmatic butcher.

Yeah, six foot, same as me, the loyal assistant butcher laughs. You want me to lay down?

The pragmatic butcher joins in with his laughter, hehehe, no longer than that! Fuckin' hell! Too long! Hahaha! Too long!

Six by two, seven inch, six hundred and fifty for the wood.

Six fifty only, says the pragmatic butcher, and with VAT about one thousand five hundred pounds.

For all of it, says the loyal assistant butcher, yeah, lots of money.

Lots of money, echoes the pragmatic butcher.

That's what they paid for that one at Stanley and Sons.

They paid for at Stanley and Sons?

Yeah about fifteen hundred.

Fifteen hundred, one thousand five hundred?

Yeah. This one's a thingy wood ennit, Canadian Rock Maple.

This one no good, says the pragmatic butcher, chop chop chop, and like that, no very hard, the wood no very hard.

Yeah yeah, says the loyal assistant butcher. Just for the block, six foot, one thousand three hundred and fifty.

Which one, this one?

The six-foot one, the long one.

Don't need the long one, says the pragmatic butcher.

The loyal assistant butcher laughs, hehehe, we could put it on top of the sink.

We don't need that long. We could just get a big plastic one, says the pragmatic butcher, just put there.

Just get the big plastic one over there, echoes the loyal assistant butcher, chop your chicken!

That one not for the chopper, says the pragmatic butcher, that one, chop over there, chop over there, you can't listen everybody, bang! bang! bang! bang! That one not for the chopper. Just small chopper, or slice.

Just slice. Hahaha, says the loyal assistant butcher, put some springs in the middle!

A woman in a black headscarf and long skirt stops at the stall with her husband. Hello, how are you? she says.

She asks the pragmatic butcher for a piece of pork loin. The bigger one, that one, no, no, yes, that one. She points. How much a kilo?

Eighteen, says the pragmatic butcher

No, no good, I can get these for fifteen pounds at the other stall. Big ones! She waves her hand in the direction of an imaginary stall.

The pragmatic butcher laughs, I always give you discount, you know that. Forty-six pounds.

Forty, says the woman.

No way! Forty-six. The pragmatic butcher does little to disguise his irritation.

Forty-five. The woman is firm. I am buying other things too. She moves to the other side of the counter and starts to order whole chickens, chicken wings, chicken drumsticks, pork bellies. The team of butchers weigh, cut and wrap the purchases for the woman.

You want the heads off? The loyal assistant butcher holds three whole chickens in his hand.

Yes, heads off. The woman nods her own head firmly and slashes one hand across her throat.

The pragmatic butcher places five bags of meat on the counter. The woman takes them and puts them at her feet.

Eighty-six, says the pragmatic butcher.

Eighty, says the woman.

Eighty-six is already discount, insists the pragmatic butcher.

The woman looks indignant. At the same time she catches the eye of her husband and points with her chin at the five bags of meat. He picks up four of the bags and stands behind the woman. She snatches up the last bag in an exaggerated display of anger, throws four twenty-pound notes on the counter, and wheels away from the stall, followed by her husband staggering under the weight of the shopping bags.

The pragmatic butcher takes the four notes and calls after the woman, I give you too many discounts!

The woman looks back over her shoulder, laughing loudly. See you next time! she shouts, waving her free hand triumphantly above her head.

The pragmatic butcher is on his mobile, speaking loudly. He grabs a pen and starts to write on his order pad. He repeats slowly but loudly the order as it is given to him on the phone. After the phone call he prepares an order, wrapping up sides of pork belly, beef steaks, whole chickens. He weighs them separately before putting them in plastic shopping bags.

Nǐ hǎo! Nǐ hǎo! Five white men in leather jackets shout greetings in mock Chinese accents as they walk by the stall. They roar with laughter. The pragmatic butcher glances at the loyal assistant butcher but says nothing.

THE PORK BUTCHER. They don't all speak English but that's no problem. There's this couple who, like, point, and I say, chopped like that? No problems at all. Everybody has a way that they're able to get across to you. Basically, if none of them could talk, we'd still get on. Sometimes it might be a lot better. Especially with the ladies. If you went back ten years ago you could actually say that about eighty per cent of our customers are Chinese, and then there was Filipinos. What you'll find is that the Chinese are dying off, the Filipinos are dying off. What's actually happened, if you go back, say ten years ago, a Chinese couple what came over in the fifties or the sixties, premature, then they open a take-away, and they're rearing children. So she would come down here, get the stuff for the take-away, and also shop for the family. They always do it on a day-to-day basis. Those people now, them children have grown up and gone. The couple now, who live on their own and are very old, they don't need so much. So it's going. They don't come any more.

A father and son are buying pig trotters. The new assistant butcher with many tattoos is serving them. Six pieces did you say? The new assistant butcher with many tattoos checks with them, picking up the pieces one by one and putting them in a blue plastic bag.

That's right, eight pounds altogether, right? The father takes out his wallet, waiting for the new assistant butcher with many tattoos to confirm the price. Do you speak Chinese? the man asks, while waiting.

The new assistant butcher with many tattoos shrugs, shaking his head.

Five pounds of chicken wings, right? The assistant butcher scoops a pile of chicken wings into another plastic bag, looking at the father.

That's right! No, no, that's enough! The man tries to stop him when he sees how many chicken wings he is putting in the bag.

To make it just right, the new assistant butcher with many tattoos explains with a grin, tipping his head to where the plastic bag sits on the electronic scales.

Oh, top man! Cheers! The man is pleased, and leaves carrying his several bags of meat.

The pragmatic butcher is separating ribs from pork belly. The meat cleaver slides beneath the ribs, and a whole layer comes smoothly out of the roll of pork belly. The pragmatic butcher is skilful, cutting with no hesitation, no planning or checking. His knife is very quick and accurate. The meat on the ribs will not be so little as to put off his customers, nor so much that he loses profit.

THE GENIAL BUTCHER. At that time we came across plenty of cold eyes and cold shoulders, and people looking down on us. A trader from one of the butcher stalls wouldn't even talk to us. Back then pig trotters were normally thrown away by the slaughterhouse. Later on, with more people starting to ask about trotters, they started to charge us for them, but they still gave them away to the English butchers for free. Some of the wholesale suppliers hid the trotters when they saw my husband coming, to get rid of him. His English sucks, we know that, so it was hard for him to argue. We couldn't do much about it. It's racist. They only give discount to Brits, but not to Chinese. But it's their loss, because they don't know how to do business. We won't do business with them, and in the end it will be their loss.

A white Transit van stops outside the window opposite the pragmatic butcher's stall. A Chinese man with a yellow baseball cap beckons to the pragmatic butcher with his index finger through the window of the van. The pragmatic butcher hesitates for a while, then goes out to talk to the man in the yellow baseball cap. The man stays sitting in the van. The pragmatic butcher rubs his hands together and stamps his feet to keep warm. His breath is visible in the cold air as he speaks. He returns to the stall and puts different kinds of meat on the scales, then wraps it up, puts it into bags, and scribbles figures on the bags with a marker pen. He asks the new assistant butcher with many tattoos to put all the bags of meat on a supermarket trolley and take them to the van waiting outside. The loyal assistant butcher comes over to help. As soon as the meat has been loaded, the van drives away.

The loyal assistant butcher has his head down, concentrating on plucking hair from pig trotters. He scrapes the hard skin and hair from the trotters with the narrow blade of a knife and sweeps all the excess into a ball. He rolls the ball in his hand and dumps it in the bin. Two points! he says, quietly celebrating his clean shot to the basket.

The loyal assistant butcher takes a phone call from the meat supplier. He ends the call and speaks to the pragmatic butcher. Enoch the pork butcher has sent back some pork loin. He said do you want them, one five five a kilo, use for mince, whatever. Four cases.
Stinky? asks the pragmatic butcher.
No, says the loyal assistant butcher, it's too fat. They can't sell it because it's too fat. Within five minutes the supplier arrives with the fatty pork loin. Oh hello, says the loyal assistant butcher, in a stylised, faux Chinese accent. Where are they?
All right? The supplier greets the loyal assistant butcher.
Is that what Enoch said, they're all right? asks the loyal assistant butcher.
What's up with them? asks the supplier. One twenty a kilo, you can fuckin' have 'em.
You just said one fifteen on the phone, says the loyal assistant butcher.
One fifty, I says, one fifty.
One twenty, says the loyal assistant butcher.
You can have them all at one twenty, twenty-five kilo, says the supplier.
What's up with them? What's wrong with that one? asks the loyal assistant butcher.
Fat? Fat? He's worried about the size ain't he? Oh that's Enoch. What is it, a hundred kilo? A hundred and twenty-five. I'll just run and get rid of these boxes.
If you want it, phone me as I'm going round, says the supplier.
If the boss says yeah I'll come down and empty it myself, says the loyal assistant butcher. What is it, just these? Let's have a look at that.
They'll get no credit for that, says the supplier.
Yeah, but it's Wednesday today, it's not your fault, says the loyal assistant butcher, it's their fault for not using it. They'd have been better off stripping that and mincing it. I'll take that. We'll just use it for mince.

A couple buy pig intestine from the Chinese-student butcher. He picks up several pieces and shows them one by one, before putting the white, greasy stuff into a shopping bag and weighing it. Five sixty, says the Chinese-student butcher. Make it six? he asks them, starting to add more pieces to the scales.

No, no, make it five! The woman doesn't want to buy more than she has budgeted for.

I will pick out a smaller one, says the Chinese-student butcher. He selects a different piece of intestine, checking the figures displayed on the electronic scale. He quickly wraps it up and hands it over to the woman. The customers pay and leave, their little girl jumping up and down behind them.

How much is your Silkie chicken? asks a Chinese woman.

Fifteen pounds, says the pragmatic butcher.

What? says the woman. It's so expensive!

The pragmatic butcher stands by his price. Tell me that after you go and look in the Day In grocery store. More than sixteen pounds. Go and have a look. The pragmatic butcher gives a shrill whistle to emphasise his point.

I'll have one then, says the woman. You hardly ever see them.

The pragmatic butcher and the genial butcher are at home, talking about the staff on the stall. Some of the assistant butchers would like to work five days rather than six, says the pragmatic butcher.

He is not happy with the new assistant butcher with many tattoos. He is off on Thursday, he works five days, paid five days, kwailo. I said to him I want to do three days myself, or two days, or no need to work at all!

The genial butcher supports him: you work, you get paid!

The pragmatic butcher continues, I want to be CEO, just sign and finish work, I want to be the president. Can I be? The ideal is different from reality, right.

Yes, says the genial butcher, no work, no money.

You don't have a choice, says the pragmatic butcher.

You don't have a choice, says the genial butcher.

THE MAN ON THE CHICKEN STALL. We've been here for quite a few years and people come to us for the quality of the meat, you know. You see these chicken breasts, the chicken carcasses, we do a lot of chicken at our stall and people come to us for this traditional English food. That's why people come back to us, you know. The thing is, about twenty-five, thirty years ago everybody went to the market. It was the only place where people did their shopping. Nowadays only people who are fed up with supermarkets come to the market. But we do a lot of chicken and people know about it. If more people came to the market we would do better. We need to find a way to attract people down here. Once they are here they will buy chicken.

On a white mannequin head, a black balaclava with an opening only for the mouth. It is topped with a flat cap. On an adjacent head, a black balaclava with an opening only for the nose and eyes. It is topped with a gold porkpie hat.

Sheep heads piled on top of each other like newly hatched reptiles appearing for the first time. Calcified eggshell and membrane clings to their noses and chins. Their teeth are prominent and clean, like sets of dentures. Some of the heads are grey and pallid, not yet warmed by the sun. Others, though, are vivid pink, already living. The largest of them is sharp as a tack, its big, round eyes ready to take on the world.

A pair of blue rubber gloves heavy on clear plastic storage boxes.
Inside the boxes hundreds of false nails like razor shells
washed up on a beach and stripped clean.

On the shelf above, bottles of nail polish and nail lacquer.
Aquamarine, bronze, old gold, copper sunset, pearlescent,
satin black, Prussian blue, mandarin, indigo.

On the top shelf a display box. In each cell of the display box
a brightly coloured nail, each one like a butterfly,
or a bird's egg collected from a remote expedition.

On the lowest shelf, a prosthetic hand, the sort that can be
screwed into an artificial arm. It is flesh-coloured.
Each finger of the hand wears a long, curved nail.

The nail on the little finger is crimson, ring finger vermilion,
middle finger mauve, index finger scarlet, thumb metallic pink.
Inscribed in large letters across the knuckles of the hand,

in permanent black marker pen, DONT TOUCH ME ... PLEASE.

老板, 有没有猪舌头卖? A young Chinese man stops at the counter and asks the butcher whether he has pig tongues, 猪舌头在外面, 他们去外面拉货喽, 五分钟就回来. The pragmatic butcher tells him they have just arrived. If he comes back in five minutes he can have them.

The Chinese-student butcher is tall, lean, and good-looking. He's skipping college today to help on the stall because the loyal assistant butcher is not feeling well. For some days he has been complaining of an acute pain in his stomach. He has nevertheless come to work. He wears a green woollen hat and looks paler than usual. The genial butcher is concerned about her colleague. She speaks quietly in Mandarin. Do you know a Chinese remedy to cure a stomach infection? He went to see his doctor but was sent away with nothing but painkillers. You know what the doctors are like here. I keep trying to persuade him to see a Chinese herbal doctor. He only ever drinks Coca-Cola, that's the problem. He needs to eat more garlic, drink less Coca-Cola. She looks at her colleague with matronly concern as he chops pork ribs.

A Chinese man looks intently at the meat on offer at the counter and eventually points to his selection, saying to the new assistant butcher with many tattoos, two kilo. He also says, chop. The new assistant butcher with many tattoos takes the meat over to the chopping board. The pragmatic butcher points to a tray of pork belly and asks the customer whether he is interested. He is not confident that the man understands his Chinese. The man shakes his head, and the pragmatic butcher says, no? He changes tack and tries to sell the man chicken. Chick-chick! The man refuses the pragmatic butcher's cheerful solicitation.

Two young men arrive at the stall. They call to the pragmatic butcher, who is in the store at the back of the stall. He comes out to see them. They have come to pick up an order. He leafs through several sheets of paper and card until he finds their order. It is written in a small notebook. He takes a calculator and spends a couple of minutes working out the cost of their purchase. The two men wait patiently.

There has been a theft of chopping boards from the stall. The genial butcher views CCTV footage at home with her parents.
You saw him? asks her father.
Yes, we saw him stealing from us, says the genial butcher.
So you know who it was?

We know, and we will make sure we take it further. He deserves it.

Her father yawns and stretches. If it wasn't valuable, what's the point?

They're thirty pounds each, she says, still angry at the violation of the theft.

How many did he steal? asks her mother.

He stole two. We bought them for thirty pounds each.

How many have you got?

We have a few, says the genial butcher.

What time were they stolen? asks her father.

Six thirty yesterday.

You have him on video? he asks.

Of course, I checked the CCTV footage. It would have been terrible if he wasn't on it.

Did he have his face covered? asks her father.

No, no, his face wasn't covered.

It's a good thing you have the camera, says her mother.

A lot has been stolen before, says the genial butcher, and now we have the evidence. She points to the screen. Can you see, he is choosing what to steal, taking two, how stupid he is!

It looks like he doesn't know there's a camera, says her mother.

He thinks we can easily be taken advantage of.

Have you approached him about it? asks her father.

Yes.

What did he say?

We asked him did he steal them, she says. He said no, that he is not that kind of person. When we showed him the evidence he said he just borrowed them to take measurements.

Why didn't he ask? says her mother.

Yes, since he didn't ask, it's stealing. The genial butcher points to the screen. You see, he's taking the chopping boards. Thirty pounds each. He brought them back today, she says.

He returned them? asks her mother.

Yes, but it's still stealing. He didn't admit responsibility. It's stealing even if he returned them.

THE FLOWER SELLER. I'm not saying it was a good thing to open the floodgates, I'm not saying that at all, but now that we have we might as well make the most of it, rather than trying to fight it, we might as well just embrace it. I don't know if that's an English sort of thing to say. You're not going to win any wars in this country. They're still going to come. You're better off embracing it. You have to believe it. There needs to be more support for the markets because it's a meeting place for people in the city.

CUSTOMER. Each Saturday I come into the market for the veg, and whatever bargain I can pick up on the butchers' counters. The best time to come is between half four and five, just before closing, when they're getting rid of all the left-over stock. Last week I got a chicken for a pound, once even a whole tray of pork chops for two fifty. It isn't always like that though. You have to elbow your way in, and even then you can end up with nothing. A bag of mince will be good enough, or a bit of pig liver. But it isn't only the meat I come for. I can't resist having a peek at the shoe stall to make sure they are still there, the shiny red shoes I have set my heart on for little Jordan's birthday. They have a satin bow on the front, and a line of paste diamonds all the way down the T. Just like Judy Garland's shoes in *The Wizard of Oz*, where she taps her feet together three times and makes a wish.

THE PRAGMATIC BUTCHER. You can make more money working abroad. But mentally, the stress and struggle is just too much. Life in your village at home, on the other hand, is like living in heaven. You can never be as relaxed and comfortable here as you are in your own country, speaking your own language. My son's English is so much better than mine, even now. I try to speak it just to make ends meet, just to get by in the job. At first I had a couple of free English lessons from the city council. I was a refugee so I was entitled to attend the lessons free of charge. But it didn't fit into my schedule. The lesson time clashed with my working hours. In my first job I was paid a hundred and thirty pounds a week, and I had to work twelve hours a day. By the time I finished work it was midnight. The English lessons started early in the morning. So I just couldn't do it. I would have had to get up so early after a long night's work. That job was in a take-away restaurant. My cousin put in a word for me. The boss was from Fujian as well, and he and my cousin were quite close. I never moaned about the low pay. But things were always tense with him while I was in that job. I was mopping the floor once, and the floor was so slippery that I fell over backwards and the back of my head hit the floor really hard. The boss just laughed, and said I deserved it. No sympathy at all. I don't know why.

A butcher in a red-striped apron and a white cap walks over to Bari Bari, the mutton trader. He leaves two large pieces of meat on the scale on Bari Bari's counter. The mutton butcher sitting behind the counter nods and shouts, thanks, mate! He lifts his hand to acknowledge the gift. The man in the red-striped apron walks away, not looking back, but raising his thumb in the air above his head.

THE LOYAL ASSISTANT BUTCHER. A lot of customers want to knock down the price. Whether you can do it depends on what meat it's on. Some of it, you can knock it down a little bit, but then if it's just customers coming in telling you they want it at that price then I'll turn around and say no. If they're polite to me, I'll be polite to them and help them, because it's better business for us, at the end of the day. If they're not nice people, or arrogant and just shouting at you, telling you what they want, then I'll tell them no. I treat people the way I like to be treated. Some of the regular customers you get to know quite well. There's a woman who always comes on Tuesdays, an older woman, African-Caribbean. When I worked on Enoch's, I knew her on Enoch's, then she started coming round here when I was still on Enoch's, and I've been around the market, then I started here. That's how we knew each other. She's eighty-six or seven, and she's had operations on her eyes. If I do anything wrong, she shouts at me. I try to help her if I can.

THE GENIAL BUTCHER. I came to the UK because my oldest sister asked me to. My sister always spoke about how wonderful it was here, shopping and everything else, and how you can earn big money. So I decided to come with my other sister to study English. I was just eighteen when I arrived. I got my visa as a language student for the first year and found a part-time job outside of college hours. The restaurant was close to my college and the hours fitted. I could finish lessons at three in the afternoon and start work at three thirty. The job was in a Chinese take-away. Working on the counter, taking phone calls, orders, things like that. That's where I met my husband. He was the sous chef.

A young couple, both wearing the dark-blue trousers and flat shoes of hospital nurses. They buy a big piece of beef steak and ask the pragmatic butcher to slice it into thin, even slices. I can try, he says, but it won't be straight. If you leave it in the freezer for a couple of hours, before it's frozen hard, it's easier to slice then.

THE MAN ON THE MENSWEAR STALL. The economy is really shrinking as well. That's the other part. The economy is shrinking. In the market there's a lot of other choice. They can get their sweets, hardware stuff, clothing, materials, the café is here, shoemaker's here, key cutter is here, everything's under one roof. Plus other things. Plus, they get a bargain as well. They're paying in the shops eighty pounds a garment. We sell them for sixty pounds. That's a twenty pound difference, but the people have an image of this market, and they don't want to pay sixty pounds. They don't want to pay sixty pounds; they want other things. It used to be that if you sell things for twenty pounds, you pay twenty pounds. These days they bargain for fifty pence, sixty pence, one pound, or lower. They want to save fifty, sixty pence, one pound as well. We don't mind to knock off fifty, sixty, one pound, but if they want to do more than that, that's a bit hard for us. That's a bit hard for us. Again, that's the market.

The pragmatic butcher and the loyal assistant butcher take delivery of the day's meat and offal. It is packed in white cardboard boxes, which are stacked on a low-loader delivery trolley in the public area in front of the stall. They open the boxes and check that the delivery is correct.

The loyal assistant butcher counts to himself. Two, three, four.

What are we missing? asks the pragmatic butcher.

Missing a spare rib, missing one box of spare rib so far, one, two, three, four, supposed to have five spare ribs, says the loyal assistant butcher.

The pragmatic butcher counts for himself, one, two, three, four, four, five. Four, it should be, that right? Heart?

Should have two hearts.

Yeah, two hearts, three kidney.

Three kidney, yeah, two hearts, that's one there, one pig neck, definitely four tails, yeah?

Yeah, four. Missing, er, oh no, we've got five spare rib, which is right, four there and one there.

What about the belly?

Ah, that's what it is, five belly, should have seven.

So missing two belly, says the pragmatic butcher.

Tail, ribs. The loyal assistant butcher briefly sings to himself as he continues to open boxes. Feet, ribs. Ribs and tails again. Spare rib, spare rib, belly ribs, pig feet, spare rib. Belly ribs, pig feet.

Behind the butcher's counter is a porcelain sink,
another larger metal sink, a cutting machine,
knife grinder, mincer, electronic till,

stacked storage boxes, water heater, electric kettle,
an open packet of hot chocolate, first aid kit,
three cartons each of a thousand plastic bags, a saw,

a red-and-gold banner with gold Chinese characters,
a poster advertising the stall's produce, also in Chinese,
nine knives on the wall.

Coats and bags hang from meat hooks.
On the counter a set of digital scales.
On top of the glass display Santa Claus in all his outfit –

red suit, black boots, red hat, white beard and whiskers.
He is playing Christmas songs on the saxophone
busting a gut to be heard over the clatter of the market.

Two Bulgarian men stop in front of the counter. They browse carefully for a long time, only speaking to each other. The older of the two is well dressed, in a leather jacket and pointed, shiny brown leather shoes, while the younger one is more casually dressed in track suit and trainers. They look like father and son. Both of them put their hands deep in their trouser pockets. The loyal assistant butcher looks at them, recognising them as regulars, and asks them, chicken, boss?
The younger man looks at him asks him if the chicken is fresh.
Fresh? says the loyal assistant butcher. He tips he head towards the supplier, who is engaged in business with the pragmatic butcher at the other end of the stall. Here's the delivery man and he can prove to you that our meat is fresh! The loyal assistant butcher grins at the man and starts to scoop chicken wings into a big, white plastic bag.

Three sixty. Three pounds sixty, says the loyal assistant butcher. He tilts the scale towards the man so that he can read the numbers displayed.
The man nods his head. His mobile phone rings and he starts to speak loudly. He stops talking, but still holds his mobile phone to his ear. He taps on the glass cover above the pork mince to show the loyal assistant butcher what he wants and holds up three fingers.
Three kilos? The loyal assistant butcher checks the order.
The man nods, still with his phone pressed to his ear.
The loyal assistant butcher starts to weigh the meat.

In the meantime the pragmatic butcher talks to the older man, who is pointing at a tray of chicken wings, and holding up two fingers of each hand.
Four kilos? Four kilos, right? says the pragmatic butcher.
The man nods.

The young man ends his phone call and points at the beef steak.
The loyal assistant butcher picks up one piece and puts it on the scale.
More, more! the man urges the loyal assistant butcher.
The loyal assistant butcher adds another piece to the scale.
The man nods and then describes a circle with each of his hands, pointing to the pork mince first then to the mincer behind the loyal assistant butcher. Same, same! he shouts.
The loyal assistant butcher turns round, points at the mincer and asks the man, you want these minced?
The man nods.
The loyal assistant butcher nods in turn, and goes to the mincer. He feeds the two steaks into the mincer as the man watches and waits.

The older man comes over and stands next to him. Now it is the older man's turn to speak on the mobile phone. He soon finishes his phone call, and walks to the other side of the stall where the pragmatic butcher is standing. He starts to order more meat. The younger man joins him and also orders more meat. Both the loyal assistant butcher and the pragmatic butcher serve the two men.

The older man points at a tray of minced pork, looking at the loyal assistant butcher until he starts to serve him.

Three fifty, says the loyal assistant butcher to the man, and waits.

More, more, the man says, so the loyal assistant butcher adds another scoop of mince to the bag on the scale.

Okay, the man says.

The loyal assistant butcher looks at the scale and says five fifty.

More, more, says the man.

The loyal assistant butcher adds more mince, but the man says, no, that's more than five fifty.

The loyal assistant butcher shakes his head at the man, not understanding.

The man raises his voice when he sees that he has been misunderstood, saying, I pay, I pay!

The loyal assistant butcher looks at him and smiles apologetically, yes, sure, he says, and starts to add more mince. Seven pounds, he says, is that okay?

The man nods and walks towards the younger man.

All together sixty-two pounds, the loyal assistant butcher says to the men.

The older man looks at the younger man, who is speaking on the mobile phone again, standing by the windowsill. The younger man nods at him and the older man takes out a roll of cash, counts out the correct number of notes and hands them to the loyal assistant butcher.

Thank you very much, the men say, as they pick up seven heavy bags of meat and walk away.

The loyal assistant butcher and the Chinese-student butcher are about to start the delivery run. They stop in front of two fully loaded supermarket trolleys beside the windowsill. The Chinese-student butcher points at the two trolleys, one smaller and one bigger, much heavier. He laughs and gestures towards the two trolleys: this one or that one? He takes the one closer to him, which is also the smaller one, and glances at the loyal assistant butcher. The loyal assistant butcher shakes his head and laughs. They take hold of the trollies with both hands and walk one after the other out of the market towards China Town.

THE MAN ON THE NAILS AND BEAUTY STALL. The city council we're fighting for two years now. Still the case is in the cold, and here and there. I don't know what they're doing. In the middle we stopped paying the access rent. We used to pay our original rent, but then again these people, they say, start paying rent, and if we will win, the money will come back again to us. They say, okay, start paying rent, but the original at the moment, not the previous. For example, the previous is twelve fifty pounds.

They say no, just pay sixteen hundred pounds, full. If we win we'll get the money back, but I don't think so that this will happen.

A tall Jamaican man with a walking stick approaches the stall. He wears a leather flat cap and a knitted cardigan. He buys three pork ribs, each of them cut into three by the pragmatic butcher, who says, three thirty, man.
The pragmatic butcher bags the ribs, saying as he hands over the bag, oxtail?
Hm?
Oxtail, any oxtail?
The man does not want any oxtail.
Six pounds thirty, please, says the pragmatic butcher.

THE PORK BUTCHER. I've noticed that Chinese students don't shop as much as they used to ten years ago, when they would be doing their own food in their rooms or in their dormitories. They would sooner go to a take-away, because they're like my children. They've grown up; mother's done it all for them. They're losing that art. I would say, if you go back ten years and compare, I'd say I have about twenty per cent less, because they've changed. Their attitude's changed. Where my own people who would come up, just walking around, shall we have a bit of steak? Are you going to cook it? And they're having a toss-up over who's going to cook it. We'll do it together. You know what I mean? Cooking, today, is a dying art, isn't it? Your youngsters, they think, well, I'm not going out day to day, shopping, I'll have a take-away or have a microwave. Eating habits and shopping habits have totally changed. My children wouldn't come to a market. They would either do it online or go to a supermarket.

The loyal assistant butcher emerges from the cold store with a large bag of pig kidney. The pragmatic butcher is serving customers. A Chinese family walks slowly by. The man pauses to ask the loyal assistant butcher for the price of a tray of pork. He holds up five fingers and says five. The family walks on.
An African man points to the kidney displayed on the counter.
The loyal assistant butcher says, that's pig.
The man says, halal?
The loyal assistant butcher says, what?
The man repeats, halal?
The loyal assistant butcher says, no.
The man leaves.
The pragmatic butcher asks, what was that?
He asked if the kidneys were halal, says the loyal assistant butcher.
Halal?

Pig, that's not halal. Is that halal? says the loyal assistant butcher.
The pragmatic butcher hits his forehead with the open palm of his hand. Fuckin'
hell, he says, and they both laugh out loud.

An old Chinese woman stops to check out the pork for several minutes before she
taps on the glass counter and asks the pragmatic butcher to give her a piece. Give me
three pounds in money, she says. He cuts a thick slice of pork loin, weighs it, and tells
the woman it is four pounds fifty.
The woman says she only wants three pounds' worth. She looks unhappy and angry,
and starts to walk away from the counter.
The pragmatic butcher is surprised at the woman's anger, and shouts after her, saying
he can do three pounds' worth if that's what she really wants.
But she is not to be reconciled, repeating that she only wants three pounds, and that's
too much. The woman continues to walk away from the stall, leaving the pragmatic
butcher to watch as she recedes into the distance.

THE WOMAN ON THE AFRICAN FOOD STALL. It's not only Africans come here. I have
customers from different countries. People come and go, you know. Even if they have
no money they still need to buy food. They try to get me to discount the prices but
I'll have no bargaining in my shop. If they can't afford it, they can leave it. Everything
here has a fixed price and I have to make a living out of it too. But by the Almighty,
please, the market will go on, it's part of the local community, and the market needs
to be here for people. But if people have no job, no money, things will always be
difficult for us. But people need to eat, so I hope it will survive.

Two women, one of them shouting loudly. She repeatedly says to the pragmatic
butcher, nǐ hǎo! He is taken aback. She also shouts, Chîne! and repeats it over and
over, pointing in the pragmatic butcher's direction. Then she shouts, ça va! ça va! ça
va!
The nonplussed pragmatic butcher looks at the loyal assistant butcher and says, I
don't understand.
The loyal assistant butcher says, ça va, I think it's French.
The woman's companion completes her purchase of pork and the pair disappear
round the corner, the louder of them still shouting as she walks on her way.

THE GOOD FISHMONGER. We are a family business and we were originally from London.
We were in London for eighteen years and we have our family shops all over London.

We run family businesses and we are brothers and nephews, and we expanded in the past few years. We now have two stalls in this market. Today we have loads of foreign immigrants shopping at our stall. I actually ask them where they are from and they tell me they are from Poland, Kuwait, Syria, Bangladesh. We have customers from all over the world including China, India, Pakistan, Thailand, Malaysia, Vietnam, Bulgaria, Czech, Netherlands, Norway, Scotland and Ireland. And a lot of people are coming from London actually. In the past few years I have noticed more and more people moved out of London to Birmingham and some other smaller cities. I think it's something to do with government policy on cutting benefits. In London the housing benefits would be much higher than what it was in Birmingham due to the house price. I have seen a lot of people are now leaving London as the government wanted to kick them out of London. A few weeks ago I went back to London and I have seen that high-class people are now living in the area where normal people used to live. I have seen a lot of that in the past few years. Birmingham is getting all the trade with people coming from those areas buying fish, and meat, and coming back to where they live and cook at home. It's good for our trade though. And with foreigners, if you want something you will find a way to make yourself understood. They've got a few words that they can say to make themselves understood. And they point and use gestures to tell you what they want. Then you always have people who want to knock down the price. I will show them the price tags here, and say, this is the price, and if they are asking for a discount I will let them know this is the discount. And they are normally okay with the price. But some people who are on a budget, they do have little to spend. They only have such and such to make a little meal, and sometimes I let them get away with it.

A well-built man with dark hair has come to the counter. The new assistant butcher with many tattoos is weighing the meat the man has chosen.
Chopped? asks the new assistant butcher with many tattoos.
The man looks at him, waits for a few seconds, and uses one hand to perform a cutting action above his other hand.
The new assistant butcher with many tattoos nods and laughs, then turns away to chop the meat. He bags the chopped meat and places it on the counter.
You have tongue? asks the man, with a strong East European accent, pointing one finger towards his own tongue, with his mouth wide open.
The pragmatic butcher picks up two huge pieces of ox tongue, and the man laughs, nodding at him, his thumb raised in appreciation of the butcher's comprehension.

THE PRAGMATIC BUTCHER. These students are all rich. They don't come here for small money. They come to kill time. To look for romance. They're all the same. Look at them in the streets, all in pairs. Three weeks after arriving in the UK they have found a partner.

I came as a refugee in nineteen thirty-six, from Berlin.
Just me and my mother. I was five years old.
I can't remember much, just the stories.

There's a fishmonger here who can get the fish I need.
He knows – pike, carp, whitefish,
has them on order every Friday.

He fillets them, separates and chops up the bones,
puts them in another bag for the stock.
Skins the fillets, takes out the pin bones, grinds the flesh.

There's nowhere else in the city you can find these fish
and no one else is so helpful.
You can't even find a fishmonger on the high street.

It's so good that I can still make gefilte fish
the way my mother taught me those years ago.
I used to come on the bus but it's too much now.

The taxi is a luxury, but why not?
The fishmonger sends one of his girls out
to make sure there's a car waiting when I'm ready to go.

THE LONG-SERVING BUTCHER. The English people now, the older generation are dying. The younger folk, they don't want to cook. Well, they don't want to go into a butcher's shop. They want to go into a supermarket, buy this, buy that. They don't want to spend two or three hours with a joint in the oven. That's what's killing the trade. You've got these ready meals, straight in there. You've got the restaurants now, go in there, two for one, saves them cooking. This is where the problem is. The English people are slowly dying, their eating habits are. Sitting round a table on a Sunday lunch, it's not happening no more, unfortunately.

The loyal assistant butcher deals with a customer complaint.
Excuse me, says the customer, yesterday I here buy goya. No good.
Goya? What's wrong with it?
Yeah, yesterday, no good, says the customer, a man with a pencil-thin moustache.
No good?
I threw it in the bin, says the man.
What's wrong with it?

It is all dark and everything, you know.

Who did you buy it off?

Here, yesterday, no good.

The loyal assistant butcher points to the fresh-looking pig stomachs on the counter.

Like that, that one?

Yeah, says the customer, no good.

You shouldn't throw it away, says the loyal assistant butcher. We can't do anything about it. If you brought it back then we can swap it. Like if you buy a TV from the shop and it's no good. You can take it back to the shop and they swap it for you. If it happens again, bring it back and we will swap it for you. But if you threw it in the bin we are not going to swap it for you.

THE MAN ON THE DELICATESSEN. Another problem we are facing is, I don't mean to sound sexist, years ago the guy used to go to work, the lady would stop at home, and every day she'd be coming out to purchase food. Now, because of the way lives have changed, unfortunately both the husband and wife are having to go out to work to make a living nowadays. No one shops on a daily basis any more.

The pragmatic butcher wears a long chain-mail glove on his left arm to sharpen his knives. First he sharpens the knives on the grinder and then finishes them with a manual sharpener. He tests the edge of each blade against his thumb and on loose ends of meat on the chopping board.

THE MAN ON THE NAILS AND BEAUTY STALL. Our nail technician works on her own, except she has wages on a percentage basis, and it's not worth that, because this is our own shop. No matter what the job is there, you've got to go for it. Before other people are getting wages, there are things, they think, okay, that's it, as soon as the customer is gone. They don't realise that we must clean the equipment and all that. From three years it's a big cost for us, so at the moment it's just best the nail technician not being here.

Two men in black leather jackets. One of them points to an oxtail. The pragmatic butcher weighs it on the scales. Four kilos, ten pound.

The loyal assistant butcher asks the men if they are Italian.

One of them points to the pragmatic butcher and says, Chinese!

He's Scottish! says the loyal assistant butcher, and they all laugh.

THE MAN ON THE NAILS AND BEAUTY STALL. My wife does threading in this room. Outside we have got jewellery. When we started the business we had nothing. We just spent our credit cards on everything. We built up slowly, slowly. It's all body jewellery up there. This we sell. The one is this selling, one is my wife is doing that, sometimes the body piercing. The nail is not there. So just basically three things are there. Just like beauty. For the threading and all that, we get middle-aged and old ladies come through here. Young as well. Lots of Chinese customers, when they come, they can't speak well. They normally point, yes, but we've got no problem for that. All Asian people, even Indians or Pakistanis, they say, how much for a pound? Can you give me two pounds? First of all, we are a market. Market means, in people's minds, market means bargain. Simple as that. I'll tell you something, if they go to Debenhams, if one coat is seventy pounds, they pick it up, go to the till, pay, head down, out. In a market anyway, the customer says, how much? Four pounds. Can I have two pounds? Yes. As a trader we say, sometimes you can't, you can't do that. If you say, not four pounds, they say can you make it three fifty. That's the last price, please. Then they say, I've got three twenty-five, is that okay? All right. Go on.

The Chinese-student butcher greets a customer, hello boss you all right? Nǐ hǎo, nǐ hǎo, nǐ hǎo.
Nǐ hǎo, nǐ hǎo, says the customer.
Nǐ hǎo, nǐ hǎo, nǐ hǎo, says the Chinese-student butcher again.
Spanish? Español? says the customer.
Why not speak Chinese, man, says the Chinese-student butcher.
I can speak Chinese, says the customer.
Hahaha, that's only one word, man, says the Chinese-student butcher, smiling.

Eel

I

I start work at six
when souls of pigs and pixies
are up to their tricks.

II

The way people leave
the public convenience
you wouldn't believe.

III

Lesley's Take-Away.
A sausage and egg sandwich
to kick-start the day.

IV

I do have a chat
with some of the stall-holders
about this and that.

V

Throw a sprat to catch
a mackerel, mackerel
to catch yellow jack.

VI

The butcher told me
to get rid of stomach cramps
drink Chinese green tea.

VII

All bloody morning
hammering on the heat pipes
no word of warning.

VIII

Health and safety, too.
It's not all about cleaning
the disabled loo.

IX

The butchers at *Chik's*
do like to take the mick but
I give them some stick.

X

She was here last week
from the university
noting how we speak.

XI

I pretend to flirt
with the girl on frozen fish
in a cheesecloth shirt.

XII

So says the gaffer:
Lutjanus campechanus
is the Red Snapper.

XIII

For gratis and free
Zsuzana from *Global Foods*
slips me a lychee.

XIV

The pungent perfume
of pig offal calls to mind
one Leopold Bloom.

XV

They sell things in here
you've never even heard of:
beef mask, caul, ox ear.

XVI

At the hardware shop
Jeyes Fluid, carbolic soap,
my nan's old string mop.

XVII

Eels in a tank like
gym freaks going nowhere fast
on exercise bikes.

XVIII

That bag of samphire
is akin to a necklace
of sea-green sapphire.

XIX

It isn't my place
to say whether people should
stick studs in their face.

XX

Doherty's fish stall
claim to have landed the year's
biggest conger eel.

XXI

He just strokes his chin
when asked the simplest method
to cook sea urchin.

XXII

The clock they restored
with four dancing figures was
damaged in the war.

XXIII

The way they rampage
through the grafter repertoire
they should be on stage.

XXIV

It's a canny squid
peddles residual ink
for three or four quid.

XXV

How splendid is that –
an impeccably dressed pig
in a porkpie hat.

XXVI

A man from Tabuk
teaches me how to say thanks
in street Arabic.

XXVII

The story I told
of a fugitive lobster
is centuries old.

XXVIII

It's green caviar
not frogspawn in pond algae.
Eat with vinegar.

XXIX

She was so chatty
I ended up purchasing
saltfish and ackee.

XXX

You'd think the sting ray
with one flap of its wings would
be up and away.

XXXI

From eyebrows to boots
a Balkan jazz crew bedecked
in red Santa suits.

XXXII

That skinny fellah
with silver eye shadow is
the fortune teller.

XXIII

The pig's intestine
is best stuffed with chopped pork lung
hartwort, garlic leaves.

XXXIV

The cats Pantagruel
and Gargantua play me
for an ancient fool.

XXXV

The worn-out leather
of her shoes testifies – heel
toe, step, together.

XXXVI

It seems a sick note
is not a sick note these days
it's called a fit note.

XXXVII

Mrs Belkedi
on the candied fruit counter
suggests fennel tea.

XXXVIII

The couple who run
the Polish deli turn out
to hail from Bodrum.

XXXIX

I take out my book
to record an incident
with a butcher's hook.

XL

Not a methane leak
but a box of durian.
Closed for a whole week.

XLI

The German market
has come to town for Christmas.
Some traders are narked.

XLII

Something to be seen:
sardines in their very own
Busby Berkeley scene.

XLIII

Today's dilemma:
a quarter of sherbet lime
or sherbet lemon.

XLIV

It didn't take long
for that Leviathan eel
to be dubbed King Kong.

XLV

She's got my number
now I've fallen for a brace
of sea-cucumber.

XLVI

At afternoon break
it is useless to resist
home-made lardy cake.

XLVII

Artisan coffee
prepared by a full-bearded
apothecary.

XLVIII

There's no way to pick
a winkle from its shell with
a winklepicker.

XLIX

I spoke to a man
said he'd walked most of the way
from Tajikistan.

L

You wouldn't have thought
mopping floors for a living
required knee support.

LI

The end of my shift
a large tub of jellied eels
I'll take for a gift.

Intestine

A customer approaches the stall and asks the loyal assistant butcher, is this pork?
Pork, yeah, says the loyal assistant butcher.
The man makes an elaborate gesture, opening his arms wide, bringing his hands together, and then opening his arms wide again. As he does so, he says, is it, erm, this?
No, no, no, says the loyal assistant butcher, you want the small intestine don't you, no, no, you want that one but the small one.
As he speaks the loyal assistant butcher points to his own stomach to represent the small intestine, and then points to the pig's large intestine, which is displayed on the counter. The loyal assistant butcher makes a sign to represent 'small' with his finger and thumb, and repeats the sign of pointing to his own stomach to represent the intestine. He shakes his right hand quickly from side to side to indicate a negative response.
The customer nods vigorously.
The loyal assistant butcher then makes a sign with his hands clasped together to represent the small intestine.
The customer repeats his original gesture twice, with arms apart, then together, and wide apart again. As he does so he says, goes long.
The loyal assistant butcher mirrors the customer's gesture with arms wide apart to represent the small intestine, saying yeah, the one that goes long but not that one, not that one, no. He points to the large intestine as he says, not that one.
Tomorrow? asks the customer.
The loyal assistant butcher shakes his head and shrugs with his hands and then with his arms, saying, no, we don't, we can't get it no more, no more, finished.
Finished, echoes the customer. He peruses alternative pieces of offal instead.

❧

The pragmatic butcher takes orders on WeChat.

Tomorrow 70 kg chicken leg with bones
20 kg pig kidney
£10 ox bones
£3 chicken offal
Tomorrow 20 kg boneless chicken wings
Tomorrow 70 kg pork belly
30 kg chicken offal
£3 ox bones
£10 pig kidney

                                          We'll send the pork belly this morning
                                                   beef belly this afternoon
                                                 is that okay many thanks

One box pork steak on Wednesday
80 kg beef belly on Thursday many thanks
Today 10 pieces pork belly many thanks
Do you have beef tendons?

                                                              no side stuff
                                                 the meat is cut off quite clean

Tomorrow 8 boxes pork belly
2 boxes beef tendon any time will do many thanks
Tomorrow 10 pieces pork belly pig heart and tongue many thanks
Tuesday 80 kg beef belly many thanks
Tomorrow 10 pieces pork belly many thanks
Tuesday 90 kg beef belly many thanks
Tomorrow 10 pieces pork belly many thanks
Today 80 kg beef belly many thanks

                                    I only have 50 kg belly here at the moment
                            do you want us to send 80 kg at 2 o'clock this afternoon
                                            or 50 kg to be delivered now?

Tomorrow one box chicken wings
sorry for the bother many thanks

A Somali man stops to buy oxtail. The loyal assistant butcher puts two pieces on the
scales. Fifteen pound. He points to the price on the digital display.
The man asks for a smaller amount.
The loyal assistant butcher replaces one of the oxtails and says, twelve eighty.
The man nods.
The loyal assistant butcher asks, do you want it cut? He makes a cutting gesture with
his hand.
The man says, yes.
The loyal assistant butcher says, here? He indicates halfway down the tail.
No, says the man.
The loyal assistant butcher replies, what, sliced? He moves his hand back and forth
repeatedly along the tail with a slicing motion.
The man nods.
The loyal assistant butcher takes the tails to the chopping board to be sliced.

THE WOMAN ON THE SHELLFISH STALL. You get different nationalities, like you would
anywhere else, really. Some customers want it a bit cheaper and try to knock down
the price. There are things you can work on, and there are things you can't. If they

buy a lot they'll want a discount, which is fine, but at the same time they've got to understand that I buy a lot, and no one gives me a discount just because I'm buying in bulk. Like I say, some things you can work on and some things you can't. Lobsters, they're dear, but they're dear for me to buy. Things do go up at Christmas. The fishermen put them up. If they put them up, I've got to put them up. I can't keep them at that same price. Christmas, what I'm usually paying for them, if I sold them for the same price then it would be the price I'm paying for them. I've got to make something, you know. I'm not here to sell it and make nothing, but at the same time we do try our best to work on what we can. I think that does bring the customers back. If you can be as helpful as you can, and work with people, and help people, then it sort of makes it a lot easier, and they'll want to come back.

A Chinese man, late middle age, points to pig hearts. Fresh?
It's all fresh, says the loyal assistant butcher.
The man points to the cold store at the back of the stall, indicating that he wants hearts out of the store.
How many do you want?
Ten, says the man.
The loyal assistant butcher goes to the store and comes back with a vacuum-packed bag of hearts.
How much? asks the man, indicating the whole bag of a dozen hearts.
Six pounds. The loyal assistant butcher puts the bag of hearts into another plastic bag and hands it to the man.

THE MAN ON THE MENSWEAR STALL. Suppose all the people that come into the market to buy meat or something else, if they buy six or seven kilograms of meat it's very hard to carry it from here to the buses or their own transport. The city council, they just want the rent and service charge, that's all they want. A lot of people are struggling, including myself as well. I'm here the last nine years in this place. I'm struggling myself these days, and the other people are struggling too. Okay, fine, people with less overheads, they can survive. People with more rents that they charge, only can survive with customers. At the moment we're just surviving because we get regular customers, but that's not a big deal. That's our heads just above water, to cover the costs. To make something extra is a bit hard. That's very hard.

An elderly African-Caribbean couple. The woman buys a piece of beef.
Do you want it chopped?
Yes.
Small? The loyal assistant butcher cuts a piece and shows it to her.

A little bit bigger, she says.
Bigger?
She also buys pork rib.
You want it sliced? The loyal assistant butcher motions with his hand.
Yes.
Ten fifty please.
Thank you.
Thank you.

A middle-aged Chinese woman says quietly, almost as if to herself, 褒汤用什么好? 要
有点肉的? She is expensively dressed in a beige suit and caramel coat. The handbag
on her arm coordinates with her clothes. Her stiletto shoes likewise. Her hair is short
and stylish. The pragmatic butcher knows exactly what she wants and efficiently
collects together the ingredients for her soup. The woman nods slightly and hands
the pragmatic butcher a five-pound note.

You came home early tonight, says the genial butcher.
The pragmatic butcher explains that he drove the loyal assistant butcher home early
because he had a pain in his stomach.
The genial butcher's father says it won't be fixed without an operation.
The pragmatic butcher points out that he didn't have an operation when he had
similar symptoms a while ago.
Sometimes you need an operation, says his father-in-law.
I saw an article on the internet that said sometimes it can be fatal, says the pragmatic
butcher.
It's fatal if it bursts, says his father-in-law, otherwise it's not fatal.

A Chinese man buys pig kidney. He is served by the new assistant butcher with many
tattoos, who wraps the kidney and hands the bag to the customer.
Three seventy, says the new assistant butcher with many tattoos.
Three seventy?
Three seventy.
Too expensive! The customer laughs.
Eight pounds a kilo, explains the new assistant butcher with many tattoos.
Oh, eight pounds.
Three seventy, says the new assistant butcher with many tattoos.
The man points to a tray of pork.
The new assistant butcher with many tattoos bags it.
Eight seventy, he says.

Eight seventy?
Eight seventy.
Eight seventy?
Three seventy and five pounds. Eight seventy.
Oh, says the customer, and hands over a ten-pound note.

The genial butcher goes to the slaughterhouse every Monday morning for pig stomachs. She can take them for free as long as she removes them from the carcasses herself. They would otherwise be thrown into the furnace. She cleans them, stripping out the fat, running cold water through the intestine again and again to be sure all the faeces are out, removing the fat that attaches to the inside of the stomach. The stench makes her sick. She doesn't do it just for the little she can make on each stomach. Word is getting round that there's a Chinese butcher in the market selling products you can't get anywhere else. The stall has started to attract regular customers, selling the small intestine, the colon, the stomach. They sell hearts at fifty pence each, while other traders sell them by weight. People from Fujian come to the market to buy pig stomach. Vietnamese customers ask for tripe. The pragmatic butcher drives to London every Sunday with two large empty suitcases, returns with them full of fish balls. The genial butcher makes advertising signs by hand with felt pens on card, in super-sized Chinese characters.

A Chinese couple want minced pork for dumplings.
How much in money? asks the pragmatic butcher.
Two pounds, says the man.
Two pounds' worth of dumplings? That will never be enough, says the pragmatic butcher.
We can't eat more than that, says the woman, the rest will be wasted.
The pragmatic butcher persists with his point, with this little bit of meat you won't make many dumplings. It's no problem if your husband doesn't want many, but your daughter will be hungry.
The woman is not convinced to buy more. We don't really like dumplings, we only make them occasionally, she says.
The pragmatic butcher stands by his argument, I didn't ask how regularly you eat dumplings. What I am saying is, how many can you make with this little bit of meat? It's enough for us, says the man, firmly.
His wife stands squarely beside him; we also have other dishes to go with the alcohol.
The man adds, I mainly eat other things with my drinks.
How does that make you full? No way! The pragmatic butcher makes sure he has the last word.

A woman is buying pork ribs. She complains to the pragmatic butcher about the way he has cut them. That's too small, I said into six!
The pragmatic butcher defends himself. Too small? You said you want small.
The customer is not happy with the pragmatic butcher and raises her voice. No, I said I wanted it cut into six! You need to listen!
The Chinese-student butcher intervenes to try to broker the stand-off. You want six pieces?
The woman moderates her tone. Yes. Please.
She turns to the pragmatic butcher and says, firmly, listen, young man, if you don't know how…. But she catches herself taking an officious tone, and laughs.
The loyal assistant butcher jokes to try to lighten things, go on, train him, you teach him how to listen, it's his fault!
The woman laughs, yes, it is his fault!

A group of four Romanian women is led by a younger woman who shops at the pragmatic butcher's stall every week. All of the women are dressed in long skirts with floral patterns. Each of them wears a sequinned headscarf, which holds in place dark, curly hair. The younger woman haggles with the loyal assistant butcher over the price of bags of pork he has filled for her. Five pounds, says the loyal assistant butcher.
She looks into the loyal assistant butcher's eyes, holding up four fingers in front of him. No, no, too much, five too much!
The loyal assistant butcher shakes his head, looking at the bags of meat the young woman has purchased. He takes the meat to the electric saw to cut it into small pieces.
Oy, half! the young woman shouts at the loyal assistant butcher.
He turns round and asks, you want them cut in half? He makes a cutting action with the edge of his right hand on the flat of his left palm.
The woman nods.

CUSTOMER. It breaks my heart, but I have no choice. I can't believe it has come to this. Fifty-five years since my mother came here. This gold is more or less the only thing she brought. She always had the idea that whatever happened at least there was the gold to fall back on. It's proper gold as well, twenty-two carat, very fine, not the sort you would find here very often. It does break my heart. There used to be help from the social, but that's all gone. My mother would have wanted me to do this. What's the point of it sitting in a drawer at home? There's a ring, three bracelets, a pair of earrings. But the necklace is the main thing. So beautiful. Set with a dozen rubies. It breaks my heart.

The loyal assistant butcher serves a man who wants to buy liver.
The man says, one and a half.
Half?
No, one and a half.
The loyal assistant butcher asks, any chicken today?
The man shakes his head.
You don't like chicken?
The man leaves, but in a minute he returns.
He buys two sides of pork. How much? he asks.
The loyal assistant butcher weighs the meat. Forty pounds.
Too much, says the customer.
The loyal assistant butcher looks at the pragmatic butcher, who pretends he hasn't heard, and continues to gaze into the middle distance. The customer concedes and accepts the price.

An African woman buys a large piece of pork belly.
The loyal assistant butcher puts two pieces on the scales.
She points to the one she wants.
He says, do you want it cut? He makes a cutting sign with his right hand.
She says, yes.
He says, here? How do you want it cut?
She indicates with her hand, an indeterminate sign which he seeks to clarify. He makes a cutting sign with his hand, and says, sliced?
She nods.
He checks by showing her a piece of pork belly which has already been cut.
She nods again, and makes two cutting motions with her hand.
He says, here and here? showing her where it will be sliced.
She agrees.
He takes the pork to the cutting board.

Every Friday afternoon I come in
for a quarter of cockles and a quarter of whelks.
This is the only place you can get them now.

You can find them in jars, pickled,
or in tins if you're lucky, but not like this.
Not served fresh over the counter.

CUSTOMER. It's no joke since they moved the bus stops. I think I'm quite fit for my age but walking up that hill past the station, or even if you go up through Debenhams, it's not like when the bus garage was round the corner on Station Street. You've always got your shopping bags on the way back, and none of us is getting any younger. So the only way I can do it now is either to buy less when I come, and really think about what I can carry, or bring my grandson. But he's getting to the point where he's got his own life and his own interests. And even then it has to be on a Saturday, and I don't really want to come on a Saturday; it gets too busy, it's better for me to come in the week. So quite honestly, what happens is, I don't come so much. My daughter-in-law will give me a lift to Tesco and I can get everything I need there, without having to struggle. It's a shame though. I like to have a chat with people and have a look round to see about bargains and that. It is, it's a real shame.

THE WOMAN ON THE HARDWARE STALL. I've been here nearly three years now. Me and my husband used to do the car boot market with the same kind of stuff for nine years, past nine years out there. Then I was out of a job and I thought, right, this is it. I want to do my own business. The kids are grown up and everything so I thought it's ideal, and that's where I really got into it. I did know all this kind of stuff. I have done a bit of buying and selling. I knew all the ins and outs of it, you know what I mean? I thought, I'll take a chance. And it's working out all right. Even though it's quiet, out of six days I'll get four busy days and two quiet days, or three quiet days and vice versa, you know what I mean? It balances out, kind of.

Two African-Caribbean women are buying sliced pork belly. They point to the pieces they want, and joke with the pragmatic butcher.
He puts five pieces on the scale.
Four ten. You want two more pieces to make it up to a fiver?
They don't reply, but he picks out two more pieces anyway.
One of the women says, I don't want a skinny piece.
He picks up a larger one.
She says, too big.
He chooses something in between, and puts the two pieces on the scale. Five eighty, but for you a fiver. How do you want them cut? He makes a gap between his forefinger and thumb.
The woman indicates the size of the piece she wants, mirroring his finger and thumb action. He cuts the meat, bags it and hands it across the counter.

THE PRAGMATIC BUTCHER. Setting up the market stall wasn't easy. It was really, really difficult. I would have given up if I hadn't been really determined. You have to be strong and hang on when things are bad. When we first started we didn't even have a car. The only transport we had was a small trolley from the supermarket. I had to go to the wholesale market with the trolley two or three times a day to get stock for the stall. To be honest, talking about it now doesn't express the pain and difficulty we went through at that time. You can only get anywhere close to how we felt by going through the whole process yourself. There was also a difficult time about a year after we opened up, when we couldn't afford to hire another member of staff. My wife had to go to the slaughterhouse to pick up stock, leaving me to man the stall on my own. When the deliveries arrived I had no choice but to leave the stall unattended and run to pick up the delivery and rush back. It was really difficult. I really don't think anyone can appreciate how hard it's been, even if you tell them all the stories. Things are much better now, but it hasn't been an easy journey.

A young couple with a small child are buying chicken from the Chinese-student butcher. He puts chicken pieces in a bag and weighs them. Six pounds fifty, he says.
The young couple are not happy.
He takes out a piece of the chicken and weighs the bag again.
Four sixty.
Still they are unimpressed. The woman customer moves over to where the chicken is displayed.
The Chinese-student butcher says, I can give you another small one.
She nods.
He selects a new portion and weighs the bag again. Five pounds.
The woman is satisfied. She hands over the five-pound note she has been clutching in her hand.

The pragmatic butcher jokes with a group of students. So he is the Finance Minister and she's the Procurement Minister! The students laugh. Are you all from Birmingham, or Aston University?
No, we are from BCU.
In Selly Oak, right?
Can we have a student discount?
You only get a discount if you make a big purchase, says the pragmatic butcher.
How much discount?
Depends how much you buy: the more you buy the cheaper it is.
Next time, then. We've bought enough for today, but we'll come to you next time, now we know you are here.
Good, good, says the pragmatic butcher, do come often!

A week until Hallowe'en
and all the scraps of beef mask have gone.
Each day now needles dip and dart
as the pieces join and take shape.

Bullock heads, cow heads, faces of heifers
will wander the streets for one night.
Last year a half-bull-half-devil
oozed fire and smoke from its eyes and nose and mouth.

Which of the fish balls is five pounds eighty-one? A woman squints at the pragmatic butcher's handwritten sign.
These two, and that one is five pounds three, says the pragmatic butcher.
What's the difference between them? she asks.
It's the quantity of fish balls in the bag, says the pragmatic butcher; one is about ten, the other about sixteen.
How do you sell pig stomach?
We sell it by weight. Eight pounds a kilo. You don't have to have the whole kilo, you can just choose one or two pieces, that's fine. Anything else?
Another bag, she says.
One more bag of fish balls. Do you need anything else?

THE MAN ON THE NAILS AND BEAUTY STALL. We're dealing with customers from different countries, people from Birmingham, from Cannock, Coventry, sometimes the London people when they come to Birmingham city centre. Sometimes Scottish people. From all sides, the people come here, because this is Birmingham, and the Bull Ring Centre is very famous. So we've got all kinds of people here. Sometimes if people, even not Chinese, even some European people, they can't speak well. From Greece and all them. When they come they can't speak well, but the language is not important. The important thing is understanding each other. You are in the aeroplane and I can't speak English, right? You are just miming. The air hostess just comes and says, do you want to have tea? Okay. I'll ask you. You see deaf people, who can't hear, who can't talk, they are still living on this planet. Even blind people. So language is not that important for us. Understanding is more important. You understand this is four pounds, okay? Sometimes I just write down on the paper four pounds and they say, okay. So we're dealing okay. No problem for any language. Sometimes if a customer comes who is Asian, if they look Asian, then we, at the beginning, we start, hello, how are you? This and that. Then I ask, what language do you speak? If they say, I'm from India, I'm from Pakistan, then I say, okay, you can speak with me in our own language, like Urdu or Hindi, carry on.

The pragmatic butcher and the genial butcher are at home. They return to the question of the loyal assistant butcher's health.

He knows his thing could be fatal, says the pragmatic butcher.

His wife agrees.

It's not appendicitis, it's the whole bowel, probably an inflammation, says the pragmatic butcher.

He doesn't have a healthy diet, says the genial butcher. Doesn't have a healthy diet. It must be bowel ulcers. He doesn't eat well, and drinks too much Coke. It's not healthy.

Pig heart, says the butcher, cheap-cheap. Normally I stir-fry with chilli, and eat it with steamed rice.

THE MAN ON THE DELICATESSEN. We're losing it in the markets because a lot of people are tending to just go to supermarkets, buying in bulk and coming away. By doing that, supermarkets have hit on that and they're selling a second-rate product to everybody. In my opinion, anyway. I'm sure they'd disagree with that. But in the market I think a lot of our customers get the knowledge. You go to a supermarket, ninety per cent of the staff aren't trained in what they're selling. There's a price, and that's your price. There's no information about it. Although the information's all on the packaging, people like that bit of banter. They like the advice. They like being able to turn round and say, what would you do with this? In a supermarket, there's nobody to ask. You pick up a packet, you haven't got a clue. You can come into a market and you can ask the butcher, how would you cook it? I've seen a recipe, what would I do with this? You get that little personal touch which supermarkets just can't give. There are too many people going through the doors, and they don't care, basically. As long as they're getting the money from you, they don't generally care.

A couple of customers buy a bag of chicken feet. The woman, who wears a red-and-yellow-patterned full-length skirt, also chooses beef shin.

The loyal assistant butcher weighs it. Two sixty.

The man interprets for the woman, who says, okay. She also buys liver for one pound eighty.

Anything else? asks the loyal assistant butcher.

The man interprets. The woman shakes her head.

Four forty altogether, says the loyal assistant butcher.

The man and woman have further discussion and the man asks, how much that one? He points to a pig stomach.

The loyal assistant butcher gives the price, two fifty.

The woman points to pieces of pork. She says, that one, no, that one, as the loyal assistant butcher lifts selected pieces to show her.

Six fifty, says the loyal assistant butcher, after weighing the meat.

The man interprets. The woman nods. Before they walk away from the stall the woman says, can I have a receipt please?

THE SHOE SELLER. I speak Punjabi and English, that's enough for me. With the customers I can communicate with signs. You want this? Too big, too small? We don't have a problem. But the new immigrants speak more English. The Romanians, the Somalians, they all speak English. I don't know whether they learn it before they come here. They can speak English. The only ones who don't speak it are some of the East Europeans.

A man buys pork rib. How many kilos do you want? asks the loyal assistant butcher, putting a side of rib on the scale.

Two more kilos, says the customer, holding up two fingers.

How many bags? asks the loyal assistant butcher.

Two or three bags, says the man.

The loyal assistant butcher chops the meat.

The customer also buys four hearts. Three for me, he says.

The loyal assistant butcher doesn't get the joke. The man repeats it, three hearts for me.

The loyal assistant butcher still doesn't understand the joke, but the interaction concludes with smiles anyway.

THE YOUNG FISHMONGER. If you look in any dictionaries you will see the definition of the word 'market'. What I've learned at the College of Food is that a market is a place that gives you space for business. So it's normal that people want a bargain. You look after people around you, and you need to make money from your trade. I tell you what, last week a customer bought from us four boxes of sea bass and six boxes of some other fish. I knocked twenty pounds off his bill because he bought so much from us. I am a give-and-take person. You treat people in the way you want to be treated. You pay me respect and I respect you as well. I tell you what, there are some people in the market, yeah, they shake hands with you when they see you, and they buy you a cup of tea and chat to you like good friends. But when you turn your back they look at your price tags and they write them down when they get back to their stalls.

A Chinese woman buys three pieces of tripe.
Six pounds twenty, says the loyal assistant butcher.
A man who is with the woman also buys three pieces of tripe.
The loyal assistant butcher weighs them. Seven twenty.

A tray eased from a beehive is like this:
pale, intricate honeycomb
waxy, rubbery, a tessellated maze
of irregular pentagons.

Scald, cauterise, boil for three hours
with fistfuls of salt until bleached
then drench still steaming and hot
with nothing but sweet malt vinegar.

The pragmatic butcher contacts his brother in China by WeChat.

> do you know the treatment for
> appendicitis?

let me search for it
who is it for?

> the Brit working on my stall
> the Western doctor here won't
> remove it for him

in China it's called lanwei yan
if it is serious the Chinese way
is to remove it with a surgical operation
is it acute or chronic?
there is keyhole surgery

A young Chinese man buys a large box of chicken wings. He asks the pragmatic butcher to open the box so that he can inspect the contents. The pragmatic butcher and the young man joke together. The young Chinese man also examines boxes of whole chickens.
The pragmatic butcher asks with his hand whether the man wants them chopped, and says, you want it chop or just like that?
The young Chinese man says he wants the chicken chopped. He continues to shop.
Four kilos, ten pound, says the butcher.

The young Chinese man is with another man and a small child. They stay near the window, away from the stall. The young Chinese man occasionally consults the second man as he makes his selections.

Ninety-two, says the pragmatic butcher. You want an oxtail to make it up to a hundred?

The young Chinese man says two oxtails would make it up to a hundred.

The butcher concedes. He tries to sell the young Chinese man another large piece of beef, but he decides he has enough for today.

THE MAN ON THE NAILS AND BEAUTY STALL. My wife, previously she used to work in this shop with the last owner. So she is basically, six years, I can say, she's working in this business. With the last owner, before leaving I spoke to the last owner and said, can I have this shop? Previously I was a taxi driver, seven years. Two thousand and ten I gave up because I had a bit of heart problems about it. So I said, I can't do anything now, let me see what to do. So the last owner, at the same time, he wanted to close his shop. I requested if I could have this shop. So honestly, he organised all the paperwork and just sent me to the city council. He got it, I got it. So it's all right. As a city council thing, hair and beauty has to be only one licence. If you want to open yourself, you can't open it here. You open outdoors, anywhere, that's your choice. But this is a good thing. You can see. You know, in here people used to be queuing for the threading many years ago. Even when we started, there used to be five or seven ladies, always here, but now one shop just opened outside the rag market. When you go out, turn right and it's just there. I think the border would be there. There. Coco, Coca, whatever. They opened it for nails. People have got too much competition. The other one, Yoshi, is just there, the nail salon. For example, if one shop is there, they're only good. Then another two or three open so everybody is picking fewer. This is the struggle at the moment. Too much competition. But at the end it's okay.

A Chinese man in a crimson tracksuit is choosing pork ribs. The pragmatic butcher asks him which piece he wants.

The Chinese man in a crimson tracksuit says he doesn't know, and asks the pragmatic butcher for help.

The second one from the bottom, says the pragmatic butcher, the second one from the bottom. I should have told you to get one from the top, because now I have to go to all the trouble of getting you the one near the bottom.

You left all the big ones at the bottom, says the Chinese man in a crimson tracksuit.

The big ones are at the bottom so that the stack of ribs doesn't fall over, explains the pragmatic butcher.

The third one looks fattier, says the Chinese man in a crimson tracksuit.

Not as fatty as that one, says the pragmatic butcher, touching the second-to-bottom piece.

All right, I will have that one.

He says he will come back later when the ribs have been cut. Do you have pig ears? he asks.

Pig ears only come on Friday, says the pragmatic butcher.

THE SHOE SELLER. I do all footwear. From babies through men's, working, fashion, high boots. I've got footwear for all the family. We've got working shoes, we've got dress shoes, leather shoes. But we are struggling very much. We need more people coming. Nobody's coming here, there's nobody to sell to. People don't come here like they used to. The money is tight with them, and it's tight with us. Even the bargain price, it doesn't make any difference. I'll tell you a story. A two-pounds pair of shoes, they say, can you save them for next week. You know, they say, five pounds for two pairs, can you save them over next week. I haven't got the money with me. There's a lot of people saying that. In other markets you're outside, and if it's raining or if it's wet, you can't trade. It's more comfortable here in the indoor market. It's like a shop. It's like a shop rather than a market. Here you pick a shoe, try it and buy. You can try them on. If there are any problems, they can bring them back and exchange them or refund the money. We try to work like a shop. We do all sorts of shoes, leather ones, boots, fashion. We've got men's shoes, I do them all. Children's shoes, baby shoes, dress shoes. Slippers. Men, ladies, children. You ask me, I'll get you the shoe. I can get you next-day delivery from my cash-and-carry people. If there's something we haven't got on here, I can order them for you. Can you imagine wellingtons for a hundred pounds? Hunter. They come here and say, I want a Hunter wellington. It's one of the top makes.

Last week one of the butchers took me in where he hangs his meat in the cold store. Two complete deer carcasses, fur still on, antlers, big brown eyes, the whole thing. It was quite something. You wouldn't see that in Sainsbury's.

THE FLOWER SELLER. Rainbow nations. Yes, I think people don't try. Us, we should try, but the ones of us who don't try, I think it's just being ignorant more than anything, know what I mean? They think that they've been doing it for years this way, and they shouldn't bother. But they should. I deal with more Africans lately, and they are hard work to communicate with because they really don't want to learn. They're quite happy being in their communities; there's enough Africans to not have to learn, if you know what I mean, in their little communities. It's nice, though. But even the way you serve has got to be different now, hasn't it, you know what I mean? Whereas before, you're just catering for your old grannies, ring and ride, and now you're catering for people who have, like, European Day and things like that. We didn't have that before, we didn't have nothing like that. I quite enjoy it, actually. I love it. I'm a travelling man, anyway. I don't do Europe, I prefer South East Asia. I get on well with them, they're really friendly. I've been to Poland and it's not a place for someone like me to be. It's really, really not. When they're here they're a bit more, you know, not so bad, but you've still got prejudice. My little boy gets prejudice. He gets called 'blacky' by the Polish lads at his school. But that's just because of the way the Polish lads have been brought up. It's not prejudice. You understand what I mean?

A young man in a baseball cap wants two whole sides of pork belly.
Separate bags? asks the loyal assistant butcher.
Separate bags, agrees the young man in a baseball cap.
The butcher puts two pork bellies on the scale and notes the price on a pad of paper. He explains why he separates the pieces of pork into different plastic bags.
The young man in a baseball cap calls to his friend, who is leaning against the windowsill. He points to something on the counter and both men nod. He gives his order.
All together? asks the loyal assistant butcher.
The man leans across the counter with his arms over the top of the glass to show what he wants. The loyal assistant butcher makes notes on a small pad of paper beside the till. He makes calculations on the electronic calculator and writes more notes on the pad. The young man in a baseball cap pays one hundred and twenty pounds in bank notes. But the loyal assistant butcher tells him that his fifty-pound note is no longer legal currency. It won't be accepted by the bank, he says.
The customer looks confused.
The pragmatic butcher calls over from where he is unloading the delivery trolley, if you have a business account you will be all right.
Have you got a business account? asks the loyal assistant butcher.
The young man in a baseball cap says he has.
He pays in twenty-pound notes and wheels away the large purchase of meat in a supermarket trolley.

THE MAN ON THE DELICATESSEN. We have regular customers, customers from all over the country who phone us on a regular basis and they pick up orders. Starting next year, we'll start doing internet orders. That part of our business is growing. That can only be good for us, and as I was saying before, we have to move on. And we have customers from other nationalities. Especially in some of the other European countries, they're used to the market mentality more. In England because supermarkets have got such a hold on us, we tend to just go to the supermarket and that's it. In a lot of different countries they are used to that market mentality. They're more used to it than we are, in some respects. Which can only be good for us, because we're learning from them. I've got customers from Romania, Bulgaria, whichever countries, and they're telling me how to cook things. They're telling me, I bought this, what would you do? I'm quite happy to take their advice. Sometimes it doesn't work. Sometimes I take it home and try it, and it hasn't worked, but that's life. At least you're getting that customer confidence, and they're happy to give that information to you.

Three women dressed in long, dark-coloured skirts with big, flowery prints and sequinned head scarves. The youngest woman is in her twenties, the other two in their mid-fifties. One of the older women is the younger woman's mother. The women are physically intimate, linking arms and laughing together. The pragmatic butcher recognises them as regular customers and starts to scoop chicken wings into a bag without being asked.
Chicken, yeah! Cheap cheap! says one of the older women loudly. Soon she starts clucking and screeching like a chicken, winking at her daughter and friend, laughing at herself.
The pragmatic butcher too bobs his head, his neck jerking back and forth to mimic the movement of a chicken, one hand in front of his head pointing forward like a chicken's beak, the other resting on his hip to represent the chicken's tail.
The chicken woman and the pragmatic butcher laugh uproariously. The daughter and the friend exchange embarrassed glances.
The pragmatic butcher finishes wrapping the chicken wings, and the chicken woman hands over a twenty-pound note. The pragmatic butcher takes it and says to her, that's all? Okay, bye bye, and walks away to the other side of the stall, apparently having ended the service encounter.
No bye bye! says the woman, still standing at the counter, holding her hand out for her change.
After a second or two the pragmatic butcher walks back to her and gives her a ten-pound note.
The chicken woman winks at the pragmatic butcher and walks to the other end of the counter, where she asks the Chinese-student butcher, in a loud, high-pitched voice, how much is this?
The Chinese-student butcher looks at her and answers in the same squeaky voice, which one, which one?
The chicken woman laughs, and continues with the affected voice, this one, this one, how much?
The Chinese-student butcher checks and squeaks back, ten pounds.
Ten pounds! Too expensive! squeaks the chicken woman. She laughs loudly and waves to her two companions. The three of them go on their way.

THE MAN ON THE CHICKEN STALL. We have a lot of foreign customers and they come back. They ask you and they give you the basic words. They've got certain words that they speak to you to make you understand. It's hard to learn all these languages at school. How many languages are they teaching at school now? You have French, German and Spanish, and that's it. You don't have the chance to learn Polish or Czech.

Two Chinese women in their twenties come to the stall with toddlers in prams. They ask the pragmatic butcher something, and one of them speaks to the loyal assistant butcher. As she is speaking, the woman raises her left hand, holding back three fingers, and bending them towards her palm so that only her thumb and her little finger remain visible. Six! she says to the loyal assistant butcher, in Mandarin. The loyal assistant butcher knows the gesture. He has seen this before, and understands how many pieces of intestine the woman wants. He picks up six pieces of long, white, pig guts one by one, and puts them in a plastic bag. He weighs them and passes them over to the Chinese woman. One ninety-nine, the loyal assistant butcher tells the woman, who hands him a five-pound note. She takes the change and leaves with her friend.

THE LONG-SERVING BUTCHER. At Christmas time, it's different. Everyone wants that Christmas joint. You don't see them all year round, but at Christmas they like to come and buy something special for one week. We say, why don't you come here fifty-two weeks of the year and buy it every time? They say, we just like it at Christmas. But Chinese as well. They like their pork as well. The numbers of English customers now are slowly dying. It's a shame.

SMOKING SHOP
SHEESHA PIPES
SHEESHA FLAVOURS
BONGS
ELECTRONIC CIGGARETTE
RIZLA
GRINDERS
LIGHTERS
ALL DAY VAPES
E-LIQUID
HOOKAH PEN
APV
CIGALIKES

THE LOYAL ASSISTANT BUTCHER. The amount of customers keeps going down and down instead of it trying to go up. To me, you've got the Bull Ring shopping centre across the road. They have adverts on television and things like that. We ask in here about adverts for the market, and the manager of the markets, he says that we've got to pay for the adverts ourselves. We think, with all the charges that the traders have got to pay, that they'd put a small advert on the telly. It doesn't help. The price is up on everything, but we've got to keep it down low to keep the customers coming. And it's hard to keep prices down when the wholesalers keep putting them up. One of our main frozen suppliers, our first order, they were like, we don't do discounts, blah blah blah. I said, all right, well if I put a massive order in, what discount can you give me? We don't do discount. I said, well I can go and phone this person instead. I had another name. All right, we'll give you ten per cent. So they gave me ten per cent off the order. I mean I'm not being horrible to the wholesale market, but the wholesale market is only supposed to be for traders, whereas now they open it up to the public as well in the morning. That's why we're losing a lot of trade in here as well. It even says not open to members of the public, but they just let them all in.

THE MAN ON THE NAILS AND BEAUTY STALL. We have got regular customers and fly customers as well. Mainly, honestly, our business is with regular customers, basically. They know who we are, how we are, what we do, what respect we're giving back, or taking and giving them. So we've got, still, regular customers. About seventy per cent, our regular customers. Sometimes when they come, eyebrow threading, okay, we're charging five pounds. Eyebrow threading at Debenhams, they're charging thirteen pounds. Eyebrow threading, Selfridges is charging eighteen pounds. Just because of the name. Otherwise they're here in vain, just the same as us. Now, Coco, they're trying us to collapse more. They start at two pounds fifty. When they opened it was five pounds, and now they put it to two fifty. So even our original customers, a few, they tried to go there. They made their eyebrow wrong. Some thing, some they couldn't take the hairs off, these things, so they came back again. What you give, you get back. The positive things you do, you excel and that helps you always. Lots of customers, they left here and they start coming back again. It's just the quality of the trade and the name. Business is business, and customers are customers.

An African-Caribbean woman climbs on to the step to get a better view of the produce displayed on the counter. It's for my dad, she says, he doesn't need so much, you know what I'm saying. She also wants a kilo of chicken feet. He's given me ten pounds in money so I'm just gonna try using that.
Six pounds forty, says the genial butcher.
I just want two ribs, says the African-Caribbean woman.
Two? Three twenty. Six forty and three twenty, so nine sixty. Okay?

The African-Caribbean woman nods.

Nine sixty. Thank you very much. Thank you very much. Take care! Bye bye.

THE MAN ON THE MENSWEAR STALL. I keep my samples in the store. If they buy anything and they're not happy, bring it back, they get a full refund. Any time. Some stores give it two weeks. My policy is, bring it back any time, get your money back. No problem. The customers, twenty per cent, we try to convince them what they want. They do their best as well, to say what they want. Some people, before they leave home they write it down, what they want. What size they want. They'll show us the paper, we'll look at the paper, it tells you. We sell to people from eighteen years old to ninety-year-old people. The older people, they get the home people to come. They don't come themselves, their carers come to us. They know what they want, they just buy. They've got a list of what they want, ABC, and they just buy and they walk off. That's like, very old people who can't walk, can't come to market, they send their carers to buy stuff. And we can order it for them. If we don't have any of it in stock we can order it. If it's a local base, we can try and get it next day or the day after. Most people, if they need anything they'll let us know by Wednesday and they'll be back again in the market by Saturday or Friday. The stuff is here for them and they're very happy about that. I'm using my suppliers for the last thirty-odd years, the same suppliers, I'm using them. It's a very old company I'm dealing with. Plus I go to new suppliers, but those ones I want take the very minimum order to look at their quality. They're online. I want to check the quality, see if the quality is worth it to pay them twelve pounds for one pair, or pay four pounds to somebody else. See if I can sell for eight pounds or sell for twenty pounds. When I deal with suppliers I'll get a minimum order, look at the quality, then go deeper than that.

A customer arrives at the stall as the pragmatic butcher and the loyal assistant butcher are dealing with a large delivery of meat. The customer wears a black bomber jacket, denim jeans, a black beanie hat, and, despite the cold weather, a pair of flip-flops.

Hello my friend, how are you? You need anything today? Cheap cheap! says the pragmatic butcher.

The man in a black bomber jacket points to pork belly.

He is served by the newly appointed assistant butcher, an older man in spectacles with a kindly face.

The customer reaches over the counter, touching the meat where he wants it cut.

Chop small one, says the man in a black bomber jacket.

Yes, says the newly appointed assistant butcher. He places one of the halves of belly on the scale, and makes repeated cutting signs with his left hand over the meat, saying, rib out?

Yes please.

The newly appointed assistant butcher weighs the meat. Six pounds fifty, he says.

The man makes a gesture with thumb and index finger.

The assistant butcher says, rib out, cut small, meat as well?

Yes please, says the man in a black bomber jacket, thank you.

The assistant butcher takes the meat to the cutting area.

The man in a black bomber jacket shouts anxiously at the newly appointed assistant butcher, who turns round to look, knife in hand. The customer raises his left hand, and says loudly, I say you cut this one! He makes long cutting gestures and says, straight like that.

The assistant butcher confirms, just cut like that?

Yes, says the customer, and nods his head. He strikes his forehead with his hand, clearly unhappy with the service.

While the customer is waiting for the pork to be cut, the pragmatic butcher tries to interest him in a purchase of ham hock. The man in a black bomber jacket asks him the price.

Three quid, says the pragmatic butcher. You want any chop? Whole one? No chop?

The man makes three small cutting gestures.

The pragmatic butcher says slowly, one, two, three, pointing to the ham hock.

But not totally chop, says the man in a black bomber jacket.

The pragmatic butcher runs his finger rapidly down the length of the hock, and says, you just slice.

Slice only, says the man. He places a twenty-pound note on top of the counter, waving it in the pragmatic butcher's direction as he does so.

The pragmatic butcher looks over to where the newly appointed assistant butcher is still chopping the pork belly. The pragmatic butcher looks alarmed. After a moment he confesses to the customer that his assistant has cut the meat into small cubes instead of slices.

Oh my goodness! says the man in a black bomber jacket.

The pragmatic butcher lifts a new pork belly from the counter display in front of him and shows it to the customer, who nods. The pragmatic butcher takes the meat to the cutting area. He speaks to the newly appointed assistant butcher, he want slice, he no want cubes.

The newly appointed assistant butcher defends himself, he said cubes, cut it small. But his account is met with silence.

Ten pounds, ten forty, says the pragmatic butcher to the customer.

The man in a black bomber jacket separates his thumb and finger to show how small he wants the meat sliced.

The pragmatic butcher lays the palms of his hands on the pork belly, with his fingers slightly spread to indicate a measurement. Like that? He asks.

The man in a black bomber jacket tips his head to indicate assent.

The pragmatic butcher puts the ham hock into a blue plastic bag with the sliced pork belly. He says, just belly, and the hock, yeah? Thirteen pound please.

The man in a black bomber jacket says, I leave twenty, eh?

The pragmatic butcher, straight-faced, looks at the man in a black bomber jacket and says, where's twenty?

The loyal assistant butcher, who is watching the interaction, laughs.

The man in a black bomber jacket says, I don't know.

The loyal assistant butcher, still laughing, tips his head and eyes towards his boss, acknowledging the joke.

The pragmatic butcher goes to the till to get change.

The customer, smiling, says, you always do the tricks! The pragmatic butcher laughs, enjoying his joke.

The man in a black bomber jacket has seen something else he would like to buy. He points to a pig stomach.

The loyal assistant butcher picks up the stomach and the man says, you give me discount?

Discount? says the loyal assistant butcher. I'll give you a free carrier bag or two!

The stall does not charge for plastic bags.

The loyal assistant butcher places the pig stomach on the scales. Three fifty.

The customer raises his thumb. He points to the pig stomachs, and repeats the raised thumb gesture, saying, good skin. Thank you very much, he says.

Not a problem, says the loyal assistant butcher, as he hands over the bag.

The man in a black bomber jacket says, take it easy.

The loyal assistant butcher says, thank you, and laughs.

Thank you!

Thank you, cheers.

Fish

THE GENIAL BUTCHER. If you are in China Town you can only target your Chinese or regular customers. It is still the market that attracts more customers, many more customers from all backgrounds. When a group of customers walks past our counter we say, here come the fish. Sometimes you can catch big fish, or lots of fish, but sometimes only tiny fish or no fish. Here in the market, one net can catch all sorts of fish. But if we were in China Town we could only catch Chinese fish.

LEMON SOLE   DOVER SOLE   TURBOT   GROUPER   POMFRET
PETTISH   SHARK   HAKE   CARP   GRASS CARP   WHITING
POLLOCK   GREY MULLET   RED MULLET   SNAPPER   SEA BASS
STONE BASS   SALMON   COD   MILTS   COLEY   HADDOCK
MACKEREL   SEA BREAM   FRESHWATER BREAM   SARDINE
TUNA   EEL   GURNARD   HERRING   LAPŢI   SWORDFISH
MONKFISH   ANCHOVY   WHITEBAIT   PLAICE   SQUID

The parrot has neither feathers nor squawk
And is unlikely to learn to talk

The goat does not graze on mountain heather
In any kind of dreadful weather

The monk prays not for eternal life
Nor does he wish he had taken a wife

The doctor will not see you now
To tend your ever fevered brow

The trumpet does not harbour dreams
Of playing the blues in New Orleans

The coffin will never carry the dead
From chapel to final resting bed

The dragon will not seek a knight
For legend's most heroic fight

The cardinal will not turn a blind eye
The cardinal will not turn a blind eye

The pragmatic butcher is stocking the trays, and stops when a Chinese man stands in front of him at the counter. The pragmatic butcher hands the man three blue plastic bags which are heavy with the meat the man purchased earlier and left at the stall. 来点儿鱼丸呗! 六包三十镑钱! says the pragmatic butcher, trying to persuade the customer to buy six bags of fish balls for thirty pounds. The man looks at him, laughs and shakes his head, 好的啦! 六包就六包! 你好会做生意, but is persuaded to buy the fish balls. The man compliments the pragmatic butcher on his business acumen as he fills another plastic carrier bag with six bags of fish balls.

THE FLOWER SELLER. There are certain people who come here. I mean, I've got a woman who comes to me, she's just learning English, and she's a lovely, lovely woman. She's learning English so she can be a part of, you know, when she comes out to the market. She's learned more of her English from talking to us than she has from her class. That's what they should be pushing for. A bit more diversity in that sense, you know what I mean? It's still segregated very much, though, because you've got a Polish man sets his stall up, he'll have all these Polish flags out there, whereas the English lads don't have English flags out there; it's like, to say, come to us, we're Polish. Do you understand what I'm saying? If you go down to Digbeth there's a shop, and you'd think it's the head of the National Front. It's just covered in red and white, just red and white flags everywhere. It's just to attract the Polish. It's not to attract the likes of us. You understand what I mean? It's to say, come in here, because we can deal with you and we can cater for you. But we can't, unfortunately we can't. If you look around the market at the stalls of the other people who are here, Polish lads there, you've got Africans there, you've got English there, Irish there. It's a nice, diverse kind of place. There needs to be more to promote it, really, to celebrate it. There really should.

A couple with a small child. The woman is dressed in a long skirt and brightly coloured blouse and a headscarf. The man says to the loyal assistant butcher, how much that? pointing to tripe displayed behind glass on the counter.
The loyal assistant butcher gives him a price, but the man does not understand, and repeats, how much?
The loyal assistant butcher puts three pieces of tripe in a bag and weighs them. Seven pounds.

The man looks unenthusiastic.

The woman points to the tripe and says, take one.

The loyal assistant butcher removes one of the pieces of tripe from the scales, weighs it again and says, five eighty.

The man nods. He asks, how much? He points to a tray of chicken.

Ten pounds.

They pay for the tripe, but do not buy the chicken, and move on.

THE MAN ON THE CHICKEN STALL. When the pound changed to the kilo there was so much confusion. People would only say oh, that's a nice tray of chicken, but when you ask them how many kilos there are in the tray, so you know the unit price, they start to realise maybe it's not a very good deal when they see how much the chicken costs in pounds.

Following the departure from the business of the new assistant butcher with many tattoos, the neighbouring fishmonger has a word to say to the pragmatic butcher. The genial butcher and the loyal assistant butcher are also at the stall.

The fishmonger, whose parents arrived in the city from Pakistan many years before he was born, has a broad local accent. He shouts to the pragmatic butcher from his position on the fish stall, his deep voice audible above the clatter of the market, where'd all your staff go?

The pragmatic butcher is hesitant in his riposte, and the fishmonger warms to his theme, you sacked 'em ain't you? he sacked 'em, he said I'm don't worry, I take them on, I sack them as well.

The pragmatic butcher responds, he sack me, I'm no sack him.

The fishmonger asks the loyal assistant butcher for an explanation, what happened to him?

The loyal assistant butcher answers, he got another job.

The pragmatic butcher elaborates, yeah, he just want do properly English meat butcher, you know he don't want do like intestine yaa yaa.

The fishmonger is outraged, his voice rising, what d'you mean fuckin' English butcher, I do butcher mate, you do everything! You do fuckin' intestines, whatever come you have to do it!

The pragmatic butcher agrees.

The fishmonger points directly at the loyal assistant butcher, see, he is a different white man.

The genial butcher joins in, he's an Asian man!

The pragmatic butcher laughs.

The fishmonger continues, he's a bit of Chinese, bit of Asian, everything, he don't mind!

The pragmatic butcher echoes him, laughing, he don't mind, hehehe.

The loyal assistant butcher says, as long as I put a smile on your face.

A fashionably dressed young Chinese man asks to buy a chicken. The loyal assistant butcher shows him two types – one he says has more meat on.
The man chooses the one with less meat.
The loyal assistant butcher says, chopped? He points to the head and feet. You want to keep them?
The man does not reply.
The loyal assistant butcher chops off the head and feet and turns to the man. Small, medium? He indicates with the gap between his forefinger and thumb.
The man does not respond.
Small? asks the loyal assistant butcher. He takes silence as assent. Small, he repeats, and chops the chicken into small pieces.

A large cart loaded with pig legs trundles by, pulled by a young butcher. He pauses to shout over to the loyal assistant butcher that he has won money on the National Lottery scratch card. Fifty quid, straight up! The young butcher grins broadly. The loyal assistant butcher doesn't reply. The young butcher goes on his way.

One of the fishmongers stops to speak to the genial butcher. No more babies? No more! she says, and laughs. Why? asks the fishmonger, with a mischievous grin. Too many, she says. Too many? You've only got two, right? Three, she says. Three? One more! Four! Four, make it four! Hahaha!!

THE BEEF SELLER. You can pick up a few words of Polish, and Chinese. Yes, Chinese. For years and years, when I was in the old market, we used to pick up a few words on the fish, because I used to do fish as well. I've done fish, I've done fruit and veg, I've done meat. With the fish, we used to get a lot of Chinese coming over, and they couldn't really speak English. With Chinese, you've got different dialects. They reckon there's fifty different dialects. What they mean by that is, like, if you go to the Black Country, their accent is different to the Brummie accent. If you go to Wales, North Wales to South Wales, they speak quicker. If you go to Ireland, they speak quicker. Parts of Scotland, you go to Scotland, they're totally different. They'll talk and you'll go, what? You know what I mean? That's, I think, the same in China. They've got the same. It's such a vast country. They've got Hong Kong. And I noticed one thing, as well. You know the take-aways and things? If you look above them, it says Cantonese or Chinese. I have actually seen it. If you look into some of these take-aways, if you look on the top, it will either say Cantonese or it will say Chinese. Why do they do that? Is it because they're from China and it's a different recipe? I've just seen it, I've noticed it. I've got a few friends who are Chinese, they buy off me chicken and that. I serve the Chinese and I serve the Cantonese. The only reason why I learned this is because they explained it to me.

PLEASE
CHECK YOUR CHANGE
BEFORE LEAVING THE COUNTER
AS MISTAKES CANNOT BE
RECTIFIED LATER

The Chinese-student butcher is chopping chicken into small pieces for a woman, who waits impatiently, asking him when he will be finished.
Yeah, yeah, he says, as he hands her the bags of chicken pieces, that's twelve pounds all together.
No, says the woman, I gave you twenty pounds earlier. I paid for that.
Oh, yeah, yeah, says the Chinese-student butcher. Sure, sure.
The woman looks displeased.
The loyal assistant butcher comes to the rescue, nodding his head towards the Chinese student, saying, he's trying to earn his Christmas bonus!
The Chinese-student butcher laughs with embarrassment, and says, sorry, sorry.
The woman smiles at them both.
The pragmatic butcher speaks to the Chinese-student butcher in Mandarin, you'd better remember this.
Yeah, yeah, says the student, sorry, she did give me twenty.
Here you go, says the Chinese-student butcher in English to the woman, this is the chicken, the hen.
This is the hen? she asks.
Oh, wait, wait, he says, flustered now. The Chinese-student butcher opens the bags to check. This is the hen, sorry, this one.
Did you cut off the heads? asks the woman.
Yeah, yeah, he says. He is relieved to see her leave.
The Chinese-student butcher says, that lady, skin off, head off, wings off, feet off, chop off the small bits, fat off, and chop into six, for this bag, for that bag.
The pragmatic butcher is sympathetic, yeah, yeah, he says, it take two year already!
Two year, laughs the Chinese-student butcher.

These tongues will not speak, not now, not ever.
How big they are lying side by side
like new-born babies;
you can almost hear them breathe.

Stippled and coarse as red sandstone
heavy as stone too. Somewhere oxen
heave slowly forward,
massive, uncomplaining.

THE PORK BUTCHER. Now it's like, my wife would never go shopping on foot. She does it online and has it delivered every two weeks. In a few years' time, you're going to have these people what are used to this kind of thing, who want it, because I don't want to say it, but the supermarkets are not catering to this. It's got to be in, out, large profits, we're not going to put ourselves out. We are suiting ourselves, our type, to these people. As long as we can do that, quality-wise, price-wise, and we get there, we're going to survive. You take any of those away and you'll finish the market. I mean, I'm not a supermarket person, but if it's a new supermarket opening I'll always go and have a look to see the layout. I'm amazed when I come away. You buy TVs in there, you buy this, you buy that. It's phenomenal. They're too big. So you've lost that closeness, that friendliness. It's a case of, well, put it there, people just take it and get out. There's no identity to it. It's quite bland.

An older African-Caribbean woman is buying chicken from the loyal assistant butcher. The pragmatic butcher and the genial butcher are also on the stall. The woman is a regular customer, well known to the stall-holders. She wears a yellow hat, a black ankle-length coat and red leather gloves. She chats to the loyal assistant butcher about the state of the roof of her house. She also complains that the chickens on offer on the counter are too skinny.
They are the skinny ones, blame the chickens, not me, says the loyal assistant butcher, they are on a diet. He grins mischievously.
The pragmatic butcher chips in, skinny one's good, fat one no good, he laughs. Hehehe! Skinny one more taste!
The woman is impatient with the butcher's market humour, and says, come on, I have to go home early.
The loyal assistant butcher knows that he can tease her, and says, lightly, all right, stop shouting!

The pragmatic butcher makes an aside in Mandarin to the genial butcher, hahaha, someone's not happy today! He turns towards the woman and greets her directly, summoning his most convivial butcher's voice, hello how are you? Myself I am just so so.
Not too bad, says the woman, civilly.
The pragmatic butcher presses on with his forced cheerfulness, hehehe, not too bad, only so so! He points to the pieces of chicken the loyal assistant butcher is weighing on the scales and invites her to add to her purchase, come on then, another one.
She shakes her head.

Okay, says the pragmatic butcher, just put it in the till, twenty pounds, skin off, yeah, that's it.

Twenty pounds, says the loyal assistant butcher to the woman.

The woman inspects the pieces of chicken selected for her by the loyal assistant butcher. He says, you choose yourself, you never like the ones I choose.

Come on, says the woman, I've only got half an hour.

The pragmatic butcher tells the loyal assistant butcher to put the chicken pieces in the bag. He turns to his wife and says, in Mandarin, she doesn't like it because it's too skinny.

The genial butcher replies, she wants the fat juicy one, she wants the ones that are like turkeys. She doesn't sound happy today, it sounds like her roof is leaking.

The pragmatic butcher comments that their roof is the same: there is a leak and the roofing insulation material is wet.

He speaks to the loyal assistant butcher. She's very angry today.

Her roof's broken, says the loyal assistant butcher, all the water inside.

All the water inside, echoes the pragmatic butcher.

He speaks to the customer again, in an attempt to lighten her mood, you want some carry bag? You need some carry bag going home, put all your money inside, make sure it's not get wet hahahaha! Put all money inside, yeah?

The woman laughs, and says she doesn't have enough money to put into carrier bags. The pragmatic butcher laughs too, and says, just turn on the heater, that might get rid of the water. It's all right, twenty-five, he says, discounting the price of the customer's purchase.

Twenty-five is all right, repeats the loyal assistant butcher, and hands the bag of meat to her.

I shall love you and leave you, says the woman.

Yes, says the loyal assistant butcher, go for your chat and then love them and leave them too.

Before she departs the woman says, it's my birthday today.

The loyal assistant butcher says, oh, happy birthday! How old?

Eighty-seven, says the woman. I'm still a young girl! She takes a step back, adopting the pose of a model in the photographic studio, or a Hollywood star on the red carpet, one hand on her right hip, her leg thrust out to the side.

The pragmatic butcher wolf whistles, and says loudly, hello pretty lady, you all right? Hahaha!

The loyal assistant butcher asks, you going to the pub tonight then?

No, says the woman, I don't drink.

You can still have a lager shandy, or lemonade, says the loyal assistant butcher.

Or water, says the pragmatic butcher.

Yeah water, says the loyal assistant butcher, cheap cheap. I'll take you out if you want! Hehehe!

Never mind, says the woman, I don't smoke, I don't like alcohol, I just don't.

The loyal assistant butcher says, I'll ask them to get water out of the tap, even cheaper, you sure?

The pragmatic butcher echoes him, you sure?

The loyal assistant butcher says, yes, fix your roof. Put on the heater.

The pragmatic butcher laughs and says, it's so wet there are all fish in my house.

The loyal assistant butcher laughs, hahaha! Got everything?

Thank you, she says, bye bye, see you next week!

Yes you will, says the loyal assistant butcher.

The woman takes her bag in one hand, walking stick in the other, her leather-look handbag on the crook of her arm. Soon she is out of earshot.

HAHAHAHA!! laughs the butcher. I only got half an hour!

The loyal assistant butcher joins in, hehehe! I need to rush, only got half an hour!

The genial butcher looks at the two men laughing hysterically. She asks the pragmatic butcher what's so funny.

The pragmatic butcher can hardly answer, he is laughing so much. Hahaha! Fucking Jesus!

I'm in a rush! laughs the loyal assistant butcher, hehehe, half an hour later!

I early go home, early go home! says the pragmatic butcher.

They continue to laugh uncontrollably, like children.

THE YOUNG FISHMONGER. You need to improvise for your business and your customers. It's all about making your customer happy. It's about people, and service, and how they are being served. Customers come back to you for your quality food and good service. You can't say everything to a new customer when they first shop at yours. You say hello, thank you, have a nice day, and sometimes it's surprising to hear how they begin to ask a lot of questions and start to get to know you and talk to you. Take this customer for example [*he nods towards a customer at the stall*]. There are five or six fishmongers in the market and this man comes to spend five pounds on salmon each week. He comes here to have a look, and then goes to the other stalls to buy beef, pork, and he comes back to us for his salmon steaks. He just trusts us. You need to give it a chance, give it a go and you look after your customers and, of course, you need to make money from your trade as well. I started working in the market since I was eighteen and people know me. I like going to Caribbean restaurants, Thai restaurants, Italian and Chinese. I always have money in my pocket, but the people there say I look after them, so they will look after me. So I don't pay much to eat there. You make friends with people and you look after each other. But you can't live in the past and you have to adapt yourself to the environment. Like those years when we were hit by the credit crunch, you can't sell T-bone steak because no one can afford to buy it. You have to adapt. Look at that guy over there [*he points to a stall opposite*]. He used to be the top man fifteen years ago, hiring fifteen or twenty people to work on his stalls. He did really well so he quit the trade to retire and have a good rest. But he had to come back after so many years and restart. The market is just like a jungle: the big lions get the big portion of the trade, and the smaller ones get the rest. You have to adapt, man.

UNLOCKING ALL PHONES
SAMSUNG
LYCA MOBILE
NOKIA
HTC
MOTOROLA
LG
SIM CARDS
BLUETOOTH HEADSETS
LAPTOP REPAIRS
CCTV

THE MAN ON THE DELICATESSEN. Some of them try to knock down the price, but they don't get away with it. I know a lot of the market traders think that's part and parcel of the market. I personally find that insulting. The price is there for a reason. I always say the price is the price. I'm cheaper than most. It's cheaper than any supermarket you're going to find. The price is there because that's what I need to charge to make a living. They try to haggle you down, but they don't succeed.

The fishmonger from the neighbouring stall comes over.
Have you come for some halal pork, eh? asks the loyal assistant butcher.
The fishmonger ignores the joke, and asks the loyal assistant butcher for some change.
Yeah, says the loyal assistant butcher, I will just have to ask the man with the key. What change? Silver?
Pound coins, says the fishmonger.
Pound coins? That's all right then, we don't have any silver. He shouts over to the windowsill where the pragmatic butcher is taking his break. Is it allowed to give him a bag of coins? Thirty pounds, yeah?
The pragmatic butcher addresses the fishmonger, do you have any twenty pence?
Twenty pence yeah, lots of, says the fishmonger.
The pragmatic butcher waves his hand, agreeing to the exchange.

THE WOMAN ON THE AFRICAN FOOD STALL. Most of the people come to market only because they are coming to the city centre to do other things. The buses have been taken away from the street here, so lots of our old customers can't come any more. Imagine the heavy shopping bags they have to carry. You just lose everybody. Also unlike those in the open market, we can't sell everything here. We can only sell stuff of good quality, and we can't do that like those traders in the open market selling rubbish stuff. Our customers come to us for the quality. If one person lowers his price you will have to go on everybody's level, otherwise no one will buy from you. And if money's tight you'll have to lower your price or people can't afford it. It's not easy, you know.

The pragmatic butcher notices that a bag of meat has been left on the counter. That bag in the middle of the counter, whose is it?
It's for the girl, says the Chinese-student butcher – the one who looks Thai, you must have seen her. She asked me to weigh this oxtail for her. I went to cut it and when I turned round she was gone. Did you see her?
Ah, that one, says the pragmatic butcher, I know, the Vietnamese girl.

THE MAN ON THE MENSWEAR STALL. We are long-standing traders in this place. Newcomers just talk nonsense, the newcomers. The older traders, some people are here over a very long time with the old Bull Ring market as well, so they can understand. The new traders are a bit hopeless – for one thing, they are mannerless, and also, they want to become millionaires overnight. They do, they want to become millionaires overnight. They think it's a gold mine, but slow and steady wins the race. You can't win a million pounds from the market overnight. You have to take some time. We are here, fine, we made money one time, and these days it just turned to muck. Seven or nine years back, this place was open on Sunday at Christmas, four weeks on Sunday, very highly received by our customers. Now it's open one Sunday, the last Sunday before Christmas. Last year, we opened, it was a good atmosphere. Again, they just could give the opportunity to open on Sunday, so why not? That's not a big deal, on a Sunday. The place is very famous to open from nine until five thirty. People think, it's five thirty, the place is shut. They don't bother to come back after five thirty, and they know the place is shut on Sunday as well. So the people who come, Sunday shoppers, they just go down as far as St Martin's Church, and go to New Street.

SWEET HERRINGS
ROLLMOP HERRINGS
FRESH JELLIED EELS
JERSEY OYSTER
MUSSELS
WHELKS
OCEAN STIX
OCEAN PINX
KING PRAWNS
KING PRAWN TAILS
SQUID
CRAYFISH TAILS
SEAFOOD SAUCE
SEAFOOD COCKTAIL
SMOKED EEL FILLETS
SMOKED SALMON
BLUE SWIMMING CRAB
ESCALLOPS
GAMBAS
CLAMS
BROWN SHRIMP
PINK SHRIMP
SEA URCHIN
CUTTLEFISH
OCTOPUS
LANGOUSTINE
COOKED CRAB CLAWS
LOBSTER
COOKED CREVETTES
BLACK TIGER PRAWN
WINKLES

THE LONG-SERVING BUTCHER. You still get some people who like their traditional cuts, which we are doing. We haven't changed anything. We're still doing the same. T-bones, chines, legs of lamb, half a leg, silverside, topside, we're still doing all of that. It's a pound a bowl. We haven't changed at all. For the other side, the foreigners, the Albanians, they're bulk buyers. They don't say I'll have two pork chops, or two lamb chops, they'll buy two whole loins, two whole shoulders of pork. That's what they want. I don't know how they cook their food. It's probably entirely different to how we're doing it, but yes, it's completely changed. I dread to see what it's going to be like in the next few years.

A small Chinese woman stands beside her two-wheeled shopping trolley. Her face is lined and darkened by the sun. Her hair is grey under a woollen cap. She does not appear to be in any hurry to go anywhere. Two men, both much younger than her, stand with their hands in their jacket pockets, two or three metres in front, but with their backs to her. A young man in a black hooded top appears, walking quickly. He briefly stands next to one of the two men and hands him a twenty-pound note, ensuring that the note is not easily visible as he hands it over. The man puts the money in the pocket of his jeans and nods his head without turning round. The small Chinese woman takes a box of a dozen packs of cigarettes from her shopping trolley and hands it to the man in the hoodie. The box is marked *Sept Wolves*. The man hurries off, out of the market hall and away down the street. A few seconds later another man arrives, hands over a twenty-pound note, and leaves with his booty of two boxes of Chinese cigarettes wrapped in a black plastic bag. There is a loud, shrill whistle from the far side of the hall. The small woman closes the lid of her trolley and saunters out of the main door of the market hall. The two men walk forwards slowly to a nearby fish stall and discuss the price of herring milts. Two market police officers walk by, one in a black stab vest, the other in a high-viz yellow jacket over her stab vest. They are wearing peaked police hats. They have airwave personal radios attached to their uniforms. They each have a notebook in their pocket and a pen. On their belts they carry a torch, speedcuffs, a telescopic baton and CS incapacitant spray. They walk on, out of the doors of the market hall, and across to the rag market. The small woman with the trolley returns to her position. The two men abandon their interest in the price of herring milts and also resume their post. A thin, wiry white man arrives, pays his money and collects his cigarettes, glancing this way and that as he disappears between the stalls. A Chinese couple approach the woman's minders. We want the ones from Korea, says the Chinese man, you know, the blue ones, long slim ones. We'll come back for them tomorrow when we have money. Two loafs for me, two loafs for her. Tomorrow? says one of the men. We will be gone tomorrow. You can get the money now. We are here for another half an hour.

THE MAN ON THE CHICKEN STALL. People come to the market for the quality of the meat and service. They come to the market for a chat. And they know each other and they know they are buying from somebody that they can trust. You don't have that in the supermarkets. We do the shout-outs to get people's attention. When you are in the market, that's how people talk; otherwise, if you stand there saying nothing, people will walk past you. But you don't always shout. It's like a machine on which you can turn up the volume when you want to attract the customers, and you can turn it down when you don't need to raise your voice. It's not being stupid; you are trying to sell your stuff. I used to have five or six people working at my stall all day every day, but not now. Supermarkets have changed everything. If a new supermarket is opening up in a certain area it will drain our business for sure. It's up to the council to decide how much they want to save the market. I know nowadays everybody uses supermarkets and I go to the supermarket to buy stuff myself. The markets will survive, but it depends on how much the council want to do something about it, and how much they understand the market.

A customer asks the pragmatic butcher for pork ribs – one jin.
One jin? The pragmatic butcher is surprised at the reference to the old Chinese unit of measurement of weight. Is one pound in weight okay? he asks.
The customer says one pound will do. He also asks for pig kidney.
Pig kidneys are over here, pig kidneys are over here, this one, says the pragmatic butcher, picking up a kidney and holding it up for the customer to see. One pound fifty. Two jin pork ribs. Do you want anything else? All together six pounds fifty. He bags the meat and offal. Thanks a lot, he says.
Thanks, says the customer.

THE FLOWER SELLER. The supermarkets are killing us. If you go to a supermarket and get everything the same price that you get in the market, you're going to go to the supermarket. We have a lot of people say, what's going on in the market? There's all 'save the markets' signs around. It's not us who are going to save it. I would quite happily work here six days a week, but you can't if four days a week there's no one coming because they can't afford to park. It's four pounds for two hours upstairs. Anything you save down here, you've lost on your car park. Everything's against you at the moment. They've even stopped the bus services through the city centre. That's a massive, massive – my mother's just died, but she would just come, get off the bus there, get on the bus there. But now you have got to walk a mile and a half through the city, up a hill, to get the bus home. You can't do it no more. So it's a shame. It's not thought out. The one department doesn't ask the other department. They just make their decision and they've got to abide by it. We're the last ones who've got a say, and it's either pay or you've got to go. If you've been here and it's your livelihood and it's all you've ever known, it's a lot to say I'm not coming in no more. You feel obliged to other people, because you've watched their kids grow up, you've watched their nans die, their mothers die, you've brought them flowers for it, and all of a sudden you're not here no more. It takes a toll. The rents are too high. If you work it out, five thousand pounds, you've got two members of staff, National Insurance, what's the butcher got to make on a piece of chicken to pay that? That deal, which he would have been giving to the customer, he can't do it no more, which is upsetting really. But my customers I've had them from birth to death, you know. From grandchildren being born and daughters being born to mums dying and granddads dying. It's getting to the point now, you're missing a generation, because they're not coming anymore, because they can go and get it cheaper elsewhere. All in one, free parking, all done. On a credit card. You haven't got that facility here.

Two young Chinese women similarly dressed in black denim jeans and baseball caps want to buy pork mince.

Mince, how much? asks the pragmatic butcher. One kilo? Three pounds seventy.

How do you eat the meat? asks the first young woman.

Open your mouth and chew it, replies the pragmatic butcher, winking.

How do you cook it? she persists.

You can stir fry, fry, or stew the meat, all sorts. Excuse me, beauty, shall I cut a bit more for you to make it four pounds? Three pounds seventy or four pounds, not much difference.

We are students, says one of the young women, we don't have much money.

The pragmatic butcher laughs, students have tons of money! How can you afford to study abroad if you don't have money? Which tray do you want?

The student asks him to choose.

It is better if you choose yourself. I will be dead if you don't like the one I choose for you!

The other student chooses a tray of pork.

Three pounds seventy, says the butcher.

Thank you, say the students.

The pragmatic butcher says, who's been nibbling at my chicken feet?

Nobody, says the loyal assistant butcher. Who wants to nibble your chicken feet?

Some of them are missing. Is there a mouse, or no?

No mouse, says the loyal assistant butcher.

&

THE EXOTIC-FISH SELLER. Thirty-two years on the same stall, thirty-two or thirty-three years. I've seen a lot of changes over the years. We were in the old market, which was over the road, which is where the Bull Ring is now. Yes, we've seen a lot of changes over the years. A lot of change in different people, different countries buying different ranges and varieties of fish. Different varieties of fish that we never used to sell before, but because of the internet and the way we get produce from different countries now, where we fly it in, where before it used to come by ship. It's here a lot quicker, so we can guarantee the freshness of the fish. So there's things like that. Also, we can shop on the internet using the Latin name, because the Latin name is worldwide. One particular fish has got one given name, where a lot of the fish have got different names which have been given by that particular country. So if they've got the Latin name then we know the variety of fish we can actually get. As I say, the technology today has moved so much that it's easier to get the fish here and the right sorts of fish as well. There is an influx of people from different countries now moving into the UK, so we can try and get the fish that they're used to buying in their own country, and keep the trade moving, so to say. We have got posters there with all the

Latin names on. So it's easy, if we're not quite sure, we go to the poster with all the Latin names, and we've got books as well. So if we can see, if we get a customer, they see a fish there that they're used to buying in their own country, then we can see and we see the Latin name and then we can go shopping to see if we can get it, get that particular variety of fish for our customers. If we can get it, we try to order it in. If it's a good sale, you know, we buy in bulk. Some fish are more difficult to get than others, depending on what species of fish it is. So yes, that's the way it works. We get fish from different countries. Sometimes we have to go to a middle man to get the produce here, but we can do that. With the internet, it's so much easier now than it was thirty years ago. We've got mobile phones, you can do it literally on your mobile phone, whereas before it was faxes and telephone calls through the night to make sure for some people, with the difference in the times. We do our best to try and get a range of different fish, like everybody else who works in the market. Everything's moved forward so quickly that it's easier now than it was.

A Chinese man in a hooded sweatshirt with University of Chicago inscribed in large letters across the front. Which meat is best for cooking Hongshao Rou? he asks.
Five-layered pork belly, says the Chinese-student butcher.
With or without skin?
It depends on your preference, says the Chinese-student butcher. This is five pounds a tray. You want this one?
The man nods.
The meat is bagged. The man hands a five-pound note to the Chinese-student butcher.
Here you go.
Many thanks.

THE GOOD FISHMONGER. Customers are all different. It's hard to say where people come from in this day and age, because you get so much influx of different nationalities, different countries, coming into the market today, but there are less white people, English people I'm going to say now, buying fish than there ever was. It's a multicultural society we're living in, in this city now. All different countries. Chinese, and we get a lot of Russian people in. The list is vast, that's all I can say. And we use good old-fashioned sign language and fingers, you know, for the price and everything else. And they haggle all the time now, because money's tight. Money's really tight. Obviously we have a lot of overheads. The council are not doing us any favours at the moment, because money is really tight. It's hard work at the moment, to try and make a living out of selling fish. Even though we're surrounded by an island, we're surrounded by water, I should say, the sea, we don't really eat a lot of fish compared to what we should do. It's easier and quicker to cook than a lot of meat dishes and things like that. It's so versatile, fish. You can do so many things with it. But we don't eat a lot of fish to what we should.

A middle-aged Chinese couple. They have been together for so long they have begun to resemble each other.

The loyal assistant butcher greets them. Hello, you all right?

The woman asks, how much is the tripe?

Five pounds, says the loyal assistant butcher.

The man points to chicken drumsticks. White, yellow, he says, commenting on the colour of the chicken in different trays. Should they be a little bit yellow like that?

They are the corn-fed ones, says the loyal assistant butcher, they are yellow ones.

Are you sure? asks the man.

Yeah, they got a big wash.

And that one is too skinny, says the man.

Too skinny? That one is on a diet. He was doing the athletics, he's running around everywhere. Do you want to choose them from here? Is that easier for you, do a tray from there? There we go, there we go! You happy now?

Happy now, says the man. Thank you.

Five pounds, says the loyal assistant butcher, thank you.

Three young men arrive at the stall. The most confident of the three is nominated to buy chicken. The loyal assistant butcher serves him.

The confident man asks, how much for a chicken?

The loyal assistant butcher tells him.

The confident man says, biggest one.

The loyal assistant butcher picks a chicken and shows him.

The confident man says, no, bigger one.

The loyal assistant butcher selects another.

The confident man looks satisfied with the selection now, and asks for another chicken.

The loyal assistant butcher chooses another, and asks, using both words and a cutting gesture with his hands, whether the man wants the feet and head cut off.

The confident man initially says yes, then says, no, only – and makes a cut-throat sign with his left hand.

The loyal assistant butcher chops off the feet of both chickens as well as the heads anyway. He bags the two chickens, and gives the bag to the customer.

One of the other men in the group is interested in buying something.

The pragmatic butcher has been watching from a distance and now gets involved.

The confident man points to chicken pieces and asks, how much that?

The pragmatic butcher says, ten pounds one kilo, eighteen pounds two kilos. There ensues haggling over the price, with the confident man making a series of offers, which the pragmatic butcher flatly refuses, always with a smile on his face. Now all three of the customers are smiling, amused at the attempted bartering.

The confident man says, one kilo. Then, almost immediately, two kilo.
The loyal assistant butcher and the pragmatic butcher bag up the chicken.

Now the pragmatic butcher says, any pork for you? He points the three men to trays of pork.
They seem interested but show the pragmatic butcher a bag of pork they have bought earlier from another stall. The pragmatic butcher says, how much that?
They don't immediately answer, so he asks again.
One of them says, three fifty.
The pragmatic butcher says that must be pig head.

The three men leave, but within a minute they are back again, looking at the trays of pork on the counter.
Cheap cheap, says the pragmatic butcher.
The customers echo him, cheap cheap, cheap cheap.
The pragmatic butcher says, very good, no fat, no bone inside there.
While the pragmatic butcher and the loyal assistant butcher are serving the three men they often smile broadly. The pragmatic butcher takes payment for the pork but continues to ask whether the men want anything more.

The confident man asks him how much the pragmatic butcher wants for all of the remaining chickens on the counter.
After some thought the pragmatic butcher says, thirty-five.
The confident man holds out a twenty-pound note.
The pragmatic butcher says, firmly, thirty-five.
Still the confident man presents the single note.
The pragmatic butcher says, three, five, very slowly and deliberately. He holds up three fingers of his right hand and five of his left.
The confident man again offers the twenty-pound note.
The pragmatic butcher draws a three and a five in the air.
Still the confident man offers the note.
Now the pragmatic butcher draws a three and a five on the inside of the glass counter.
The confident man continues to present the twenty-pound note.
The pragmatic butcher says, no, thirty-five.
By this time the negotiation has become something of a game, a performance, with smiles all round.
The confident man finally puts an end to the fun, and the group leaves, leaving a big grin on the face of the pragmatic butcher.

With the worn, narrow blade of a long knife the butcher trims the membrane from between the toes of chickens, each foot attended to dextrously and efficiently, then tossed back into the tray to lie with its companions.

A woman in a long dirty cardigan, full-length skirt and bottle-green headscarf lifts a torn and crumpled Tesco bag onto the glass counter with both hands. The bag is heavy. She strains under its weight. Her face looks as though it has been preserved in peat for centuries. Most of her teeth are missing or broken. She starts to take coins out of the bag, putting them on the counter. Her fingers are arthritic. She places each coin with care, counting them out in neat columns of pennies, twos, fives and tens. When she has set all of her coins on the counter, the pragmatic butcher counts them with her. Ten, twenty, thirty. Now the pragmatic butcher takes the coins and counts again as he drops them into his till. He leaves some of the coins on the counter. He gives her a ten-pound note. The woman scoops the remaining coins into her plastic bag. I'm really doing you a favour you know, he says. The woman smiles and shakes her head. The pragmatic butcher smiles too, and shrugs. The woman goes on her way.

The loyal assistant butcher is serving a Chinese couple. They want a whole side of pork belly.
He lifts the heavy piece of meat onto the counter to wrap it and gives them a broad grin. With these muscles I'll be all right! The three of them laugh as he pulls back the sleeve of his shirt and flexes his bicep.

Two women in headscarves, long skirts, cardigans and striped socks stop at the stall. One is older than the other. The pragmatic butcher, the genial butcher and the loyal assistant butcher are on the stall. The women buy a large bag of chicken wings. They also want to buy a hen, but are unimpressed with the price. The loyal assistant butcher holds up a hen in two hands, stretching it from end to end.
Look at the size of that! he says.
The women buy the hen.

Now a young man appears and joins the women. He starts by asking the pragmatic butcher how to say good morning in Chinese. How do I greet good morning?
The pragmatic butcher says good morning.
The young man says, no, in your language.
Now the pragmatic butcher understands what is being asked of him. Zaoshang hao, he says.
Zaoshang hao, says the young man.
Zaoshang hao, says the pragmatic butcher again.
Zaoshang hao, says the young man again.
Ah, says the pragmatic butcher, confirming that the greeting has been learned, and that the impromptu lesson is at an end.
Zaoshang hao, says the young man one more time.

The young man now bends forward with the upper half of his body, sticks out his bottom, and extends his left arm and the forefinger of his left hand out behind him. Everyone laughs. The loyal assistant butcher understands that the elaborate mime represents the young man's request for pig tail. Oh, the tail? he says.

However, the pig tails have not yet been delivered. They will arrive later in the morning.

The loyal assistant butcher says, I gotta wait for delivery.

The pragmatic butcher mimes with his hands driving a car, and says, car coming later.

The genial butcher says, delivery coming later.

The pragmatic butcher adds, driver.

The loyal assistant butcher says, eleven, eleven o'clock, picking up a small mantel-piece-style clock from its usual position next to the till and pointing to it.

The customers echo him, eleven, eleven.

The loyal assistant butcher laughs, and says, yeah, walk around, come back.

The young man wants to know whether it is all right for him to leave his purchases at the stall and return later to pick them up. He says, I leave it here everything?

His wife adds her voice, saying, I buy, leave here.

Before he leaves the scene, the young man asks how much his purchase of meat has cost so far. Twenty-six so far, the loyal assistant butcher replies.

The older female customer says, that's too much. However, she does not pursue the point.

The pragmatic butcher turns to the genial butcher and nods towards the women. This must be her mum, he says in Mandarin, this must be her mum, she's a spitting image of her. He turns back to the customers, and addresses the man, your wife's mum? No, her sister? His joke is a compliment to the older woman.

The young man says, not sister.

The loyal assistant butcher picks up the pragmatic butcher's cue, pointing to the pragmatic butcher and saying loudly, my brother, this one my brother, he's my brother, yeah, hahaha!!

Everyone laughs again.

The pragmatic butcher says to the loyal assistant butcher, are you going to go for your dinner? I'm all right, says the loyal assistant butcher, I don't need to eat, I'm English, hehehe, just smoke.

THE GENIAL BUTCHER. Mei is the character for Meili and Yan for Xianyan. This is how people name their girls where we come from. It is Hakka pronunciation, different from Mandarin. Taiwanese and Cantonese spell their characters in their own way as well. 陈 in Mandarin is Chen in Pinyin, in Fujian it is Tan, in Cantonese Chan. If you say Chen you are from mainland China, Tan from Fujian and Chan from Guangdong or Hong Kong. Zhou in Mandarin is Chew in Hakka or Chaozhou. When I was small, many people shared the same surname, but with different spellings. You can tell the origin of people's ancestors from the way they spell their names – Chaozhou, Hakka or Malaysia.

A regular customer, an African-Caribbean man, no longer young.
Hey, boss! he greets the pragmatic butcher like an old friend.
How are you, mate? the pragmatic butcher responds.
Not as good as you, not as good as you, says the no longer young man.
The pragmatic butcher begins to tease him, one week, you coming, next week, missus coming!
The man laughs, yeah! hahaha!
The pragmatic butcher pursues his line, always one coming! Hehehe!
He moves two trays of pork steaks towards the man, which one, one, two, two tray?
Huh! Oh dear! Tell me about it. The no longer young man is overwhelmed with the responsibility of having to decide which tray of meat to purchase.
Yeah, says the pragmatic butcher, that one, bigger one, but only six piece, that one, smaller, seven.
The customer looks at the two trays with a serious expression on his face. More, seven?
Yeah, says the pragmatic butcher, you will choose bigger one, six.
Relieved to have the decision taken away from him, the man agrees, yeah, the bigger one, the bigger one's all right, it's better.
Not certain that he should put himself entirely in the hands of the pragmatic butcher, however, he checks. Weigh the same? Same weight?
Yeah, confirms the pragmatic butcher, same weight.
The pragmatic butcher wraps the meat.
I believe you, says the man. Very quiet again, eh?
Yeah, says the pragmatic butcher.
Ne-v-er mind. The man sympathises, drawing out extended vowels. Got to get better soon.
The pragmatic butcher says, better soon, Christmas.
The no longer young man takes him up, oh Christmas, yeah, then you'll be very busy.
The pragmatic butcher tips his head towards the loyal assistant butcher, laughing, only then I will pay the man money!
Hahaha! laughs the no longer young man. Thank you, he says, and departs.

A young man is stopped by an old Chinese woman who is dragging behind her a black shopping trolley. The young man listens to the woman and then looks inside her trolley. The young man nods his head. She takes a bunch of wild chives from her trolley, slips it into a plastic bag which she takes from her pocket, and hands it to the young man. He squeezes a coin into the woman's hand and heads towards the shellfish stall.

The Chinese-student butcher is on the delivery run to restaurants in China Town. He wheels a supermarket trolley piled with meat and offal. He goes into one of the restaurants. It is two o'clock in the afternoon and the restaurant is open to diners. There are half a dozen people eating at tables. Good afternoon, says the Chinese-student butcher to a Chinese waiter, how are you?
The waiter recognises him and nods, but is too busy to stop. He disappears through a swing door into the kitchen. The Chinese-student butcher sits down to wait.
Hey, hey, hey! A diner at the nearest table to where the Chinese-student butcher sits. The diner has a broad local accent and severe haircut. There are four men at the table. The detritus of a heavy lunch litters the linen tablecloth. A dozen empty bottles of Tsingtao beer stand in irregular formation.
Hey, hey, hey, says the Chinese-student butcher uncertainly, echoing the diner.
The diner says, what's er, I love you in Chinese?
The Chinese-student butcher is taken offguard.
Uh, he says to the man, wo ai ni.
The man mimics him, woaini. Say it again, he says.
The Chinese-student butcher repeats it, wo ai ni. Wo means me, he says, ai, ai.
Woeni, says the diner.
Ni, says the Chinese-student butcher.
Woeni, says the diner.
Ni. Wo ai ni, says the Chinese-student butcher once more.
The drunken diner throws up his hands, ah, it's hard ennit, it's hard, man, you'll have to teach it.
The Chinese-student butcher says, I love you is not hard.
Another man at the same table joins the language lesson. His thick arms are heavily tattooed. How do you say suck me up and down? he asks.
The Chinese-student butcher laughs nervously. We don't, we don't curse people like that in China, he says.
Say if I met a nice Chinese guy and I say I want to suck you up and down, says the second diner.
The Chinese-student butcher laughs, you'll never, no, no, no, he says, that's wrong.

The pragmatic butcher's mobile phone rings. He is drinking a large plastic beaker of tea. There is an overwhelming smell of disinfectant. A Chinese man buys four bags of liver for twenty-five pounds. The pragmatic butcher ends his phone call and speaks to the customer. Their conversation is loud and forceful, but punctuated with laughter.

The pragmatic butcher puts the liver in a Tupperware box for the man, making an exaggerated show of smelling the empty box first and replacing it with another.

THE PORK BUTCHER. I do like interacting with customers all the time, and the chat. I get to know all the problems they have, their illnesses, I'm not very well, I've got this. And if I have the sort of lady what's looking like she's going through the change, you know, how do you know about that? Well, I'm living it at home. I know the signs. You have to have that patter with these people. You know what I mean? Some of the butchers will be shouting out to the customers, and some of the stalls it's a quieter approach. I don't really have to shout because they actually come to me anyway. You know what I mean? It's a case of, don't shout! We don't need any more trade. We've got enough on our plate.

A Chinese woman in a pink hat is looking at pork chops.
Hello, says the loyal assistant butcher, you want that one? You want all of it? The loyal assistant butcher begins to chop the pork, while the Chinese woman in a pink hat watches.
She turns to the pragmatic butcher and says, in Cantonese, hi boss, please help, tell him to cut off more fat.
The pragmatic butcher translates the request for the loyal assistant butcher, she want to take the fat off like that brown lady, that one.
Yeah, says the loyal assistant butcher.
She want that one, says the pragmatic butcher.
The pragmatic butcher serves another customer.

Mince, mince, says the Chinese woman in a pink hat.
The loyal assistant butcher confirms her request, mince? Mince, but no fat?
The Chinese woman in a pink hat addresses the pragmatic butcher again in Cantonese, please help me, cut a little bit of fat off, that's it.
The pragmatic butcher reassures the customer, he has done it, he has minced it for you. He knows, I have told him already.
The Chinese woman in a pink hat says, no, no, no, a little bit more.
The pragmatic butcher says to the loyal assistant butcher, take a little bit more fat off, and then mince.
Yeah, says the loyal assistant butcher, mince all of it, yeah?
The pragmatic butcher checks with the Chinese woman in a pink hat, mince all of it?
Yes, mince it, mince it.
All of it? asks the pragmatic butcher.
Again the Chinese woman in a pink hat repeats her request, please help me, cut a bit of fat off.
Yes, says the pragmatic butcher, both pieces need to be minced, right?

Yes, confirms the Chinese woman in a pink hat, please help me, cut a bit of fat off, I want some of the fat, only a bit off, don't cut too much.

The loyal assistant butcher understands her request, and confirms, take a bit of fat off.

The pragmatic butcher also reiterates, take a little bit off.

The woman watches the loyal assistant butcher carefully as he chops the meat. Enough, enough, she says to him, in Cantonese.

Yeah, he says, and mince all of it? Do you want it washed? Wash? Washing, yeah?

THE WOMAN ON THE HARDWARE STALL. I have my regular customers. The majority of the butchers here come to buy everyday things like liquids, bleach, black bags, hosepipe and hoses; the butchers are always breaking down on things. It's very handy for the majority of people in here. Most of the food stalls in here come and buy disposable gloves and stuff like that. Everybody works friendly with each other, it's like a whole big family. You do spend more of your time here than with your family. With neighbours, they're very helpful. Especially, the majority of us are by ourselves, kind of. So if we need to rush to the loo or for a cup of coffee we'll cover each other. It does help out. Everybody is helpful and they do help out. The majority of my customers are Chinese. If it wasn't for them I wouldn't probably survive here. For that reason, because the majority of them can't speak English or can't understand everything, for that reason I've stuck a Chinese sign there on the stall. It does help, trust me. It does help. If they don't speak English they bring pictures on their mobile, or it's on the mobile and they ask me. I do it like that, or sometimes they explain. You know, if they want a face mask they say they want masks. And they use their hands and gestures. Things like that, you pick it up.

The genial butcher, the loyal assistant butcher, the Chinese-student butcher and the pragmatic butcher stand behind the counter, no customers in sight, arms folded like Edwardian butchers posing for a photograph. Very slow, says the pragmatic butcher. He goes for a walk around the market. No busy, he says to himself. He returns to his stall. Others no busy, he says. Too quiet, says the loyal assistant butcher. Too quiet, says the pragmatic butcher.

The loyal assistant butcher sings quietly.

> It's cheap cheap cheap
> it's cheaper than we wanted it to be
> 老鸡 laoji laogei

The genial butcher is on the stall today. A small Chinese man takes a long time to select his pieces of pork fillet. She fills three bags for him. Fifteen pounds, she says.
Fifteen pounds? says the small Chinese man, feigning incredulity.
One, two, three, says the genial butcher, tapping each bag with the flat of her hand as she counts. Fifteen pounds.
The small Chinese man reaches for his wallet.
We can make it twenty if you like, says the loyal assistant butcher with a grin.
Cheeky, says the small Chinese man.
Never cheeky, says the loyal assistant butcher.
Very cheeky young man, says the small Chinese man. He and the loyal assistant butcher laugh.
Thank you, says the genial butcher, smiling.

THE BEEF SELLER. The fish name, we used to have fish names, zhong ying. Do you know what that is? The names of some of the fish? Snapper is bi yu. You pick up words for different fish. When someone comes up, when I used to be on the fish here, I'm trying to remember, because my mind's gone now. When they used to come up, they used to come up and some of them couldn't talk English, so you'd name the fish. You know, the lads, when I used to work with them, they knew. There's a lad there, his name is Richard. I don't know if he's here. He's been at the market, not as long as me, he's five years after me, and he worked on the same stall as me, but he's still on the fish down there. Sometimes he'll tell you the fish names. He'll explain a little bit of Chinese to you, what he knows, Cantonese. He works more with the Chinese on the fish. So you have to learn that, because they eat a lot of fish, don't they, the Chinese. We get a lot of, is it Romanians who eat a lot of pork? Then some of them won't. You get a lot of Polish who eat pork, and Latvians, Romanians, they all eat pork more than anything else. Chicken and pork. They don't really touch the beef. Mainly chicken and pork. It's really weird. The English want chicken fillet, they won't have the wing. Then you'll get the Africans up and they want that salted beef. There's a big thing in London we get at the moment, smoked beef. You have to adjust to your customers. You might get somebody quite well-to-do, quite well-spoken, you have to adjust to them. If they can relate to you, you can sell to them. A lot of butchers' shops, they don't know what them are, it's called chicken baps. They used to have these. That's what they have, they have the chicken baps. It's good, it's cheap food. You find that a lot of Jamaicans they will eat that, yes, they will eat it.

It was a hundred and twenty-eight pounds eighty, says the Chinese-student butcher to the pragmatic butcher. I put in the till a hundred and thirty pounds, including my own money of one pound twenty.
One twenty? says the pragmatic butcher.

That's right.

One pound twenty donated to the stall, all right! jokes the pragmatic butcher.

The Chinese-student butcher chuckles. Buy me a Coke later, okay?

The pragmatic butcher and the loyal assistant butcher have a quiet moment to clown around. They create an impromptu role-play in the voice of a customer and a trader.

The pragmatic butcher says, ten pounds? cheap cheap.

Five pounds, says the loyal assistant butcher.

Five pounds? half price, says the pragmatic butcher

Two pounds, says the loyal assistant butcher.

Two pounds? Okay, I give you three pounds, keep the change.

THE MAN ON THE DELICATESSEN. It's not a problem with communication. The language of money speaks volumes, doesn't it? They know exactly what the price is. They know what they want. They can't always explain what they want to do with it, but you give them the price and they know exactly what they want to pay. If they're happy with that price, you manage, don't you? If we go abroad on holiday, we manage, don't we? Hopefully, while you're talking to people their English becomes better. If they're going to stop in the country it's obviously right. They should learn English. But we try to provide what people want. I go on the internet a lot and find out the speciality of different countries, find out what people like, and ask the customer, yet again. If someone comes to me and they want something, they might say, can you get, or, have you got. And I say, leave it with me, I'll see what I can do. Hopefully they will come back, and if I've got it they have the confidence in me, and say, well, hang on, if I want something, I know where I can go for that. That works. That's working well. That's why we're keeping our head above water and trying different things.

Next time I will buy pig stomach and pig head, says a Chinese man in a leather flying hat.

Pig stomach, pig head, I will remember, says the pragmatic butcher.

And I always wanted to eat pig ear, says the Chinese man in a leather flying hat.

I have no pig ear today. They will be delivered on Monday morning. You want pig head?

The Chinese man in a leather flying hat makes his purchase and picks up his bag of pork steaks. I am going, he says. Remember that.

The pragmatic butcher grins, I will remember. I will definitely remember that.

The Chinese man in a leather flying hat laughs. Write it down on a piece of paper and stick it on your forehead, so you can see it every day when you look at yourself in the mirror.

The pragmatic butcher laughs. I don't need to look in the mirror, because I already know I am smart.

Ah, as if! Okay, I'm off.

Okay, says the pragmatic butcher. Thanks very much. You check the mirror every day because you know you aren't smart.

Oh, says the Chinese man in a leather flying hat, really? He is not laughing now.

Yeah, says the pragmatic butcher, so I don't need to check the mirror. He laughs. The Chinese man in a leather flying hat leaves.

THE LOYAL ASSISTANT BUTCHER. We used to have lots of Romanians on a Monday and Tuesday. We've still got a few, but many of them, when we're down there at the wholesale market putting orders in for the day, they're all down there. Buying it from down there. So we're losing out on the money. They're still making their money, but I believe if they stop serving the public again down the wholesale, then we'd order more from the wholesale to sell to the public. The way it should have been. The way it used to be years ago, but now they've opened it up to the public. To buy from the wholesale, you're supposed to have a licence from a shop and everything, you say, this is my shop, blah blah blah. All the paperwork. Like, do you know Kilroy's wholesale, as well? You've got to have ID of your own shop and everything, to go in there and get a card and everything. We've complained, but it's still the same. I think that's why they're closing the wholesale market and moving it. By the end of next year or the beginning of the year after it will be gone. There's a few plans in the mix to build down there. They're moving it to Star City, I think. That's going to put the prices up for us, for it to be delivered here then. It's one of those. Are you going to be winning more or losing more, or is it just going to stay the same?

A group of three men and two women arrives. One of the men is ushered forward by the others. I want to speak to the boss, he says, heavily, I like to speak to him. The group looks at the meat on the counter. They take more than five minutes to hold a conference on the question of whether to make a purchase. Finally they leave empty-handed.

THE LONG-SERVING BUTCHER. They always want to knock down the price. Always knock down the price. We do a reduction anyway, straight away. If something's forty pounds I'll say give me thirty-five. They'll say, I'll give you thirty. I'll say I can't do that. They're always trying to knock the price down. And if they're very good customers, which we have, we give them a bit of leeway. We tell them, look, there's the price on the window and we've already knocked a lot of money off. Sometimes, at the end of the day, when you've had it all day, it can get to you. You can get a bit grr! You can get a bit frustrated at the end. One customer out of a hundred might just cop the brunt at the end of the day. You just lose it a little bit. We try to be fair with them. Some of them do take the Michael a little bit and they want it for next to nothing. We just say, we can't do that. You're having it for less than we paid for it. I wouldn't be in business otherwise. You know? I don't mind giving you a bit of the profit, but I'm not giving you less than I paid for it. There's no point being in business.

We first used to come when we were courting.
We'd be out of the office at lunchtime
and order half a dozen oysters.

They'd shuck them there and then, dress them
put it all on a plate, lemon, vinegar,
salt if you wanted it, Tabasco sauce.

We'd stand there in the middle of the market
like Lord and Lady Muck
sucking fresh oysters out of the shell.

An elderly Chinese man with the cracked skin of a long-time heavy smoker.
Hello, he says to the loyal assistant butcher.
The loyal assistant butcher knows him as a regular customer, and smiles. The elderly Chinese man with cracked skin wants to buy pig hearts. He taps on the glass counter without speaking.
The loyal assistant butcher picks up ten hearts one by one, turning each slowly to show him. The hearts glint in the fluorescent light.
The customer nods.
The loyal assistant butcher wraps the hearts in paper, and then in two plastic bags.
The elderly Chinese man carefully places a ten-pound note on the counter.

Every Monday morning this man nods
to a plastic ice-cream tub
and holds up gnarled fingers and thumbs:
ten pig hearts for five pounds.

When the butcher weighs each heart in his hand
and turns it to the light
it shimmers like a creature washed up
still wet from the sea.

THE EXOTIC-FISH SELLER. I was here for half past five on Saturday morning, and we left at six o'clock on Saturday night. A long day. A lot of hours go in. People don't see what goes on, because we have to get the fish, we have to load it in, we have to display it, clean it, slice it, depending on what variety of fish it is, and then obviously the market opens at nine o'clock and then when the market closes we have to clean up. Everything has to be packed away and tidied and scrubbed and everything else that goes with it.

The pragmatic butcher is on his mobile phone to a customer from a Thai restaurant. Hello, he says, who's speaking? Erm, this week no, but next week.
The telephone customer says, next week?
Yeah, says the pragmatic butcher.
Um, all right then, says the telephone customer.
Okay, bye bye.
There is no one else at the stall, either colleague or customer. In the privacy of his own company, the pragmatic butcher rehearses the phone call, representing both his own voice and the voice of the caller.
Hello, he says, who's speaking? Hello?
In the stylised voice of the telephone customer: hello.
In his own voice: who's speaking?
In the telephone customer's voice, more strongly accented, and very slow: I am from Thai.
His own voice: Okay.
Telephone customer's voice, still thickly accented: have you got any bird today?
His own: no.
Emphatically: Fuck! Too loud!

THE PORK BUTCHER. It's quiet now. You'll find now, it used to be busy when it's just turned nine o'clock when the old uns used to get on the bus. But that's stopped now. So you can see there's a clientele gone there. It gets busy at about eleven o'clock now, so you've lost them hours, and then it gets busy then up to half past four. Where before, you always had pensioners who used to get on the bus to use their passes, bang, that's when we had our first wave. Then you had the offices, the dinnertime rush and then the afternoon. Everything's changing. Nothing stands still. It's got to change. It's got to survive. You can't take it away because it's part of it, it's inbred within the community. And the history. You take that away, you take the market away, you're going to lose a big part of your inheritance. You know, it's all to do with history, and if you lose that, you've got no future. It's like the railway stations.

❦

An older Chinese woman with silver hair asks the pragmatic butcher where she can buy mutton. She is in the country temporarily to support her granddaughter, who is at medical school. She comes regularly to visit, having brought up her granddaughter herself. Whenever she's here, she cooks three meals a day for her granddaughter, and invites her granddaughter's housemates to share the meals. They are studying in the same class. She hopes her Chinese dishes will prompt them to help her grand-daughter while she is away.

The pragmatic butcher cranes his neck and points to a stall in the next aisle. Mutton is red, like beef, he says. You need to go to the stall at the end of the aisle.
The older Chinese woman with silver hair is confused. The pragmatic butcher's Fujian-accented Mandarin is not easy for her to understand.
He tells her she will find fresh mutton at the stall owned by a man with a Middle Eastern face. I look Chinese, he says, the owner of the mutton stall looks Middle Eastern. He is a cha, an Indian.
The older Chinese woman with silver hair thanks him and sets off in the direction of the mutton stall.

Several minutes later the older Chinese woman with silver hair returns in consterna-tion following her encounter with the mutton butcher. She complains, it took so much effort to buy the mutton. She is not sure whether she has bought the right thing. The pragmatic butcher has little sympathy for her. How much effort is required to buy a piece of mutton? You don't need special strength to go shopping in the market. But the woman is upset. She was not able to find the right words to speak to the mutton traders. They did not understand her and she did not understand them. She tried to say she wanted to buy leg of lamb, but she didn't know how.

The pragmatic butcher looks in her shopping bag. Yes, it's lamb all right, what's the problem? You got your mutton. Did you go to the stall at the end of the aisle?
Yes, says the older Chinese woman with silver hair, I told them I didn't want the sheep's head, I wanted the meat on its body, but the butcher didn't get it. I said I didn't want the sheep's head. She says again and again that she wanted the meat from the sheep's body, the meat on its body. Oh, what an effort, she says. Don't you sell mutton here?
No, there's not enough space, he says, no room to display any more meat on the counter.

The woman shows the pragmatic butcher how she tried to communicate with the mutton traders. She stands unconvincingly on one foot, lifts her other leg, and taps her thigh three times with the palm of her hand. That's how I tried to tell them what I wanted, she says.

The pragmatic butcher can't help laughing. You used body language, I see! Body language! His face creases with laughter. Hahahaha! They can't understand that, can they? You wanted meat from the body, but all they can see is an old woman standing on one leg, tapping her thigh! Hahahaha! You wanted meat, I would have pointed out the meat for you. Hahahaha! They thought hahahaha I am so pretty, pretty! You are dead gorgeous! Hahahaha!

The woman picks up her bag of mutton and leaves, frowning with irritation and disappointment that she found no sympathy or support from the pragmatic butcher.

The pragmatic butcher turns to the loyal assistant butcher, who has been looking on, his Mandarin not sufficient to have followed the woman's tale of woe. She's say you get lamb meat, says the butcher, she see the lamb head over there being sold by the Asian men, you got, you got any any any say Chinese, yeah, language and she go lamb I want here, I want here! I say is it somebody say, like, I'm I'm any pretty? The pragmatic butcher makes an exaggerated dumb-show of the woman's attempt at body language, lifting his leg and stroking his thigh suggestively. Like that, hahaha! Hahaha!

The loyal assistant butcher laughs along.

The pragmatic butcher continues to laugh, if you know how to say it, you just say any goat, lamb meat? Yeah? That, that, that easy!

Milk

The genial butcher is at home. She hardly slept last night, having woken at around two o'clock with an idea to export baby milk formula from the UK to China. She tells her mother about her plan.

I worked out thirty-five pounds for six tins, including delivery, customs and so on. You buy your milk powder, that's it. Thirty-five pounds for the shipping charge, that's about five pounds eighty for one tin, plus eight to ten pounds. In China the price of milk powder is over three hundred yuan each. My cost price would be one fifty, about half of the selling price. So this is it, my only other cost would be the shipping charge, not including the milk powder itself.

Her mother is sceptical. It can't be that cheap.

The genial butcher persists. I would pay the shipping only, thirty-five pounds to ship six tins. You can buy the milk powder at the same price, seven ninety-nine or nine ninety-nine, so I thought this would be worth doing.

Would it be worth doing? says her mother. Is milk powder really expensive there?

Yes, says the genial butcher, even the ordinary stuff is over two hundred yuan, and you don't really know whether it has been poisoned.

The pragmatic butcher is talking about the Chinese-student butcher. He's so good looking, no wonder there are so many bees round the honey pot. But in the first place, I thought the girl he was interested in was the one who was laughing so loudly.

We didn't see who it was, says the genial butcher.

I thought it was her, says the pragmatic butcher, then I could see it was the other girl when they exchanged phone numbers. I've never seen that before

The genial butcher teases him, when you took him on did you fancy his good looks?

No, says the pragmatic butcher, I just saw him and thought he is quite good. It's the first time I have seen a girl go after a boy for a phone number, though. She fancies him. To be honest, a lot of girls don't fancy guys who work here. Chinese girls see butchers as an aggressive bunch.

She probably just fancies his good looks.

Did you ask why she fancies him? asks the genial butcher.

Just that he's quite good looking, he looks honest, hard-working, willing to work, says the pragmatic butcher.

A Chinese man asks the butcher if he has any pig trotters in stock.
Sure thing, says the pragmatic butcher. We have pig trotters, chicken trotters, but not duck trotters.
The man laughs and says he will have four pig trotters.

A quiet moment on the butcher's stall. There are no customers to serve for now, and the genial butcher, the pragmatic butcher and the loyal assistant butcher are discussing a birthday party to which the loyal assistant butcher has been invited.

The pragmatic butcher asks his assistant whether he is going to the party.
I dunno, says the loyal assistant butcher. He seems unenthusiastic about the prospect.
The genial butcher reminds him that he has already said that he will go.
The pragmatic butcher encourages him: it's free beer, he says.
The loyal assistant butcher says he worries about the cost of going to the party.
The genial butcher says, uh? you got free beer, no?
No, says the loyal assistant butcher, pay for your own beer.
The genial butcher repeats, her voice rising with astonishment, pay for own beer!
The pragmatic butcher finds this hard to believe. He seeks confirmation from his wife, got free beer?
No, says the genial butcher, no free beer, pay for their own beer.

The pragmatic butcher still remains to be convinced that this can be so. You pay? he says.
The loyal assistant butcher confirms, you gotta pay your own beer, yeah.
The pragmatic butcher once more indicates his surprise, and asks, uh? you pay yourself?
The genial butcher intervenes in Mandarin to confirm for her husband that the loyal assistant butcher has to pay for his own beer.
The pragmatic butcher responds in the English vernacular, fucking hell!
The loyal assistant butcher reiterates, pay for your own beer.
The pragmatic butcher once more asks, pay yourself?
Yes, says the loyal assistant butcher, pay to get there, pay for drinks, buy Clive a drink, then pay to get home. Many money.

The genial butcher interprets for the pragmatic butcher, telling him in Mandarin that the loyal assistant butcher must pay for everything including travel to and from the event.
About a hundred pounds, says the loyal assistant butcher.
A hundred pounds, repeats the genial butcher, in English.
Plus babysitter, says the loyal assistant butcher, a hundred and twenty.
Will you go by yourself or with family? asks the genial butcher.
If I go by myself it will be cheap cheap, says the loyal assistant butcher.

The pragmatic butcher, still reeling from the news about having to pay for beer, asks the genial butcher, in Mandarin, whether such occasions are always like this.

The genial butcher says she doesn't know. She asks the loyal assistant butcher, the birthday invitation is like this, pay for your own beer?

Yeah, he confirms.

The genial butcher emits an exasperated sigh, British!

The Chinese then, if you get a birthday invitation they pay for you? asks the loyal assistant butcher.

Pay for everything, says the genial butcher. If you invite somebody to the restaurant you pay for everything. If I invite you to my birthday party, if I invite you to my home to have a party, then we cover every drink, buy everything, buy beer, and then you just have a drink and enjoy yourself.

The loyal assistant butcher laughs. English now, hehehe, if you get invited to, like, your house, you gotta take beer, wine, present.

You have to buy the present, of course, but you don't have to bring beer, bring wine, says the genial butcher.

Right then, says the loyal assistant butcher, laughing again, I need to get some more Chinese friends, hehehe!

THE PORK BUTCHER. I've seen some changes. That's the frightening part. If we all come to this, and become faceless people where we don't interact when we go shopping, we're going to lose a big part of our identity. What people need is to be able to talk, touch and relate. You take that away and we've lost everything. This is like, you know, the last outpost, you could say. You can go around supermarkets. Any store I go to, I always go on the person that's serving me. If I think you have good service, I'll compliment you. They can make you relax or they can get your back up.

A woman asks the pragmatic butcher for bones for soup.

T-bones? he says, T-bones will arrive this afternoon. They are on the way here and will arrive this afternoon, about two or three. It's a long drive here.

What time? asks the woman.

Monday about three o'clock, a bit earlier on Tuesday, and Wednesday afternoon about two o'clock.

I came today mainly for that, she says, but it won't be here until three o'clock in the afternoon?

The pragmatic butcher smiles, go shopping for a while, and come back this afternoon. If you want I can save some for you.

The woman pauses, how about tomorrow?

Tomorrow, says the pragmatic butcher, if you come tomorrow I will save some for you.

Tomorrow what time? she asks.

Any time tomorrow to suit you, says the pragmatic butcher. I will save some for you.
How many do you want?

About six, she says

Six pieces, I will save them for you then. If you don't come tomorrow I will sell them.
What time tomorrow is suitable? she asks.

What time suits you best?

About three o'clock.

Okay, fine, see you then.

THE WOMAN ON THE SHELLFISH STALL. We usually rely on our old-time English
customers, regulars, and Chinese customers now, mainly. I started a month after
the market moved here. The difference trade-wise is quite shocking. Market days
are technically supposed to be Tuesday, Friday and Saturday. You couldn't class a
Tuesday as a market day anymore, really. Considering we still get fresh deliveries
daily. You really rely on your Fridays and Saturdays now, but even those, compared to
years ago, when on a Friday you could never walk down the aisles. It was hustle and
bustle, whereas now you've got, really, you rely on Easter and Christmas. Christmas
tends to get you through the first few months of the year, really. I mean, trade-wise
it has slowed down a lot. I don't think New Street Station's helped, with the way
that is at the minute. I think when that reopens and they open the roads coming
back into the market. They took the bus off as well, because there used to be a bus
coming down and they took that off. It's quite a walk now, especially for some of
the older generation that have to walk down with their trolleys and stuff like that.
I've walked down to New Street, it's about a ten-, fifteen-minute walk, and that's for
me. So if you've got trolleys and shopping bags and things like that, people won't
do it anymore. Especially when you've got supermarkets around every corner and on
every street now. Price-wise, you can't really compete with them, but they don't sell
the best stuff. It's just a case of trying to get people back in here now. They know the
food's good. It's just a matter of convenience, really. Parking in town, it's not cheap.
Hopefully, once everything's reopened, I mean, I think the tram will help a lot. That
will bring them down. It's just a case of getting the customers back into town. If we
can get people more into town and maybe get some cheaper parking or a new bus run
then it will bring them in, but something's got to be done to get those people in. Like
I say, Christmas, they'll come down at Christmas, they'll make the effort to come
down. So they know where we are and they'll make the effort at Christmas because
they want the stuff. So it's just a case of getting them in throughout the year. But we
have a laugh, we have a joke, everyone knows each other. We'll help each other when
we need it. The management, city council-wise, it could be better. Some things are
fine, like your security and things like that. It's just more management. Cleaning
people, they're fine. It's just management, and management on top of management.
They have to go through that many people before you actually get a result, that's
something we need to work on as well. The council don't seem to work with the
traders that well. They need a bit more communication.

No customers, says the pragmatic butcher. It's too quiet.

There is a rich smell of cooked food. Is that the smell of your lunch? asks the genial butcher.

No, says the pragmatic butcher, it's next door's lamb curry.

The genial butcher says, I will cook curry for you next time. Don't eat the lamb curry, eat the rice I brought for lunch.

Ah?

Don't eat the lamb curry.

Doesn't matter, says the pragmatic butcher, I can drink some beer with it to cool it down.

The genial butcher looks at him, cool it down, you do need to cool it down, or you'll get more acne coming out on your face.

The pragmatic butcher smiles grimly, my youth stays with me forever! It's no good for me though, it's true, all these new spots on my face every day.

THE WOMAN ON THE AFRICAN FOOD STALL. My regular customers are mainly African, but many people who are not African want to know more about African food. They are willing to try different things. I ask people to come in and have a look. Some people just want to try it and they ask you about all sorts of stuff. Sometimes they don't know the names of certain foods and ask me. I tell them the names and ask them to repeat it, so they know. Next time they come they tell me they know the name because I taught them.

Three people, one woman and two men, are being served by the loyal assistant butcher.

How much?

Nine twenty.

The genial butcher is at the chopping board and turns to ask, all right?

The customers point to the loyal assistant butcher to indicate that they are being served.

Another group passes by and they greet the first group. A large man with tailored facial hair asks the first group what they bought. After a brief discussion, the man asks the genial butcher why there are no pig stomachs.

She holds up a pig stomach and says, there are these, but the new stock will come next week.

The second man suggests to the first group that they buy the stomachs, but they move on.

A Chinese woman and man with a pushchair ask for pork ribs.

The pragmatic butcher says he will cut a new piece for the woman, and asks whether she wants ribs with more meat or less meat.

Either is fine, she says. With some meat.

He leaves some meat on, and checks with her that it is not too much. You can't cut the joint bone, he says, that is the part with the best bone marrow in it.

She agrees.

Three pounds forty, he says.

Going out shopping in the rain today with the buggy? asks the pragmatic butcher.

He doesn't want to sit in the buggy, says the Chinese woman.

He'll have to walk on his own then, says the pragmatic butcher.

A couple of steps later he will ask to be carried though, she says.

He's too heavy to carry now, isn't he? Does your son play with you? asks the pragmatic butcher, addressing the woman's husband, does your son play with you?

Sometimes, says the man.

Sometimes?

He wants me to tuck him in at night, says the husband.

So he likes to play with you, says the pragmatic butcher. My son doesn't. My son doesn't want to play with me. He says I don't want to play with you! I don't want to play with you! The pragmatic butcher laughs.

The Chinese-student butcher has an accident with a meat cleaver and has to go to hospital. While he is in hospital, the pragmatic butcher keeps tabs on his progress through WeChat.

How is it going?

I stayed at the hospital last night,
am waiting for surgery today.

do you know the time of
the surgery?

not clear, waiting to be called
by the doctor

did those two girls stay with you overnight?
a good thing we brought some bread over

no no once my bed was sorted they went
it's true that it's lucky we had bread here

they should provide food in the hospital,
see what the others have got and ask them

Okay

so you still have to stay in
for another two days?

probably

so you are living in a three-star hotel
for three days without paying
has your girlfriend come to visit you?

haha my girlfriend is on her way

girlfriend? did you make your move?
and did she agree to date you?

not yet, but watch me try today

today is Single Sticks day
let's see how you celebrate
the festival today

haha, at least one thing can be sure
that I am not single any more

THE MAN ON THE DELICATESSEN. Some things we get in, they don't work, so you don't get them again. You change it over again and change something else. Your range is constantly evolving. I think it makes it interesting as well, because you get regulars that come in every week. I'll get customers that have been coming here for the last six or seven years, every single week. They'll come here every week because they know you've got something different. Let's try this this week, let's try that. That keeps interest. It keeps you interested in the counter, it gets people thinking, well, let's see what he's got this week. That's the key, isn't it? Getting people to return. If they come in and spend a pound and we don't see them again, yes we took a pound, but we want people to spend two or three pounds every single week, go away happy and hopefully then tell a friend, I went into the Bull Ring market, spoke to the trader on the deli counter, had this, had that, had the other, he was really, really nice and something different to do each time, and it's affordable. I try not to be greedy. I try to work it so that the prices are as competitive as possible. Our biggest seller is hams. We do a lot of hams on the bone at Christmas. Whole hams on the bone. Big pork pies. More so now, smoked gammon hocks and smoked bacon hocks. We do five times as many smoked as we do plain now. For the Polish and Romanian, mainly. We've got a specialist smoking company in West Bromwich. They've got their own smokehouse so everything is properly smoked rather than painted. Proper smoke.

Two hours later the pragmatic butcher picks up the interaction on WeChat again, after the Chinese-student butcher has been in surgery.

how are things? have you told her?
don't you have any updates for us?

operation just finished
will come for a check-up the day after tomorrow
we are progressing well, I think
we are getting on really well

you forget all about us when
you have your girlfriend around

how come I forget you?

I sent you a message at one o'clock
after your message
but got nothing from you since then
doesn't that prove that you've forgotten us?

I was still on the operating table at one
I only came out at four

have you touched her hand?

not yet … on the way

still in hospital?

just come out, getting ready to go to hers

don't lose your virginity

The genial butcher asks her mother to take her daughter to the clinic for an appointment.
Mum, are you able to take little sis for her injection on Friday? I'll ask Tung Tung's mum to take you.
The pragmatic butcher asks why she booked the appointment on a Friday. Why didn't you book Tuesday, Wednesday or Thursday?
The nurse is only there on Fridays.
There's only one nurse?
Yes, says, the genial butcher, the clinic's very small and always fully booked.
But the grandmother is uncertain about taking her granddaughter to the clinic, saying she doesn't know what to say. I don't know anything, she says, how can I go?
I'll write it all down, you can take the paper with you, says the genial butcher.
Grandmother recruits grandfather to accompany her. This means that all three children must go to the clinic, as there is no one else to look after them.
What time? asks grandmother.
Ten o'clock, get there before ten and you'll be finished by ten thirty, says the genial butcher.

The pragmatic butcher is always looking for other business opportunities. But it's the timing, he says; sometimes you just don't have the time to do further investigation of what might be possible, especially when you don't have enough staff. He says he will cross that bridge when he comes to it.

The genial butcher is serving on the stall. She speaks to a Chinese woman with bright yellow gloves, who is looking at chicken pieces on the counter.

These drumsticks have fatty skin, says the genial butcher. It's personal taste. It's totally up to you; either you like them or you don't. You can buy them to make Hainan chicken rice. Do you know how to cook it?

The Chinese woman with bright yellow gloves says she doesn't know how to make it. It's really easy, says the genial butcher, Hainan chicken rice. Take this, two kilos, five pounds. Hainan chicken rice is the easiest thing to make. Just drop it in the rice steamer and cook it together with the rice.

The Chinese woman with bright yellow gloves looks uncertain. It's because we are northerners, she says.

Northerners! says the genial butcher, you don't know how to cook. You can stew it. How would you cook it?

The Chinese woman with bright yellow gloves says, slow cooking with soya bean sauce and sugar.

Slow cooking with soya bean sauce and sugar, repeats the genial butcher. It's tastier with a bit of bone. That is too meaty.

The genial butcher bags some chicken drumsticks for the woman. As the Chinese woman with bright yellow gloves pays, the genial butcher notices her wristwatch.

Your watch, is it Rolex? How much? Three thousand, five thousand?

The woman says she bought it in Korea.

You bought it in Korea? What's the exchange rate for pounds in Korea?

The woman tells her.

The genial butcher says, too expensive! Too rich!

The Chinese woman with bright yellow gloves says, my mum loves shopping at your stall the most.

Ah thanks, says the genial butcher.

Honestly, says the Chinese woman with bright yellow gloves, she says Chinese need to support Chinese.

The pragmatic butcher's brother in China is on WeChat.

Can you still use your PayPal?
I want to transfer some money to you

how much do you want to transfer?

can sis-in-law receive my messages?

yes I can

sis-in-law, your brother still hasn't added me to his WeChat
add me to his QQ as well

THE PRAGMATIC BUTCHER. Chinese are too protective of their kids. It's our tradition that we need to save up not only for ourselves but also for our children. I read from the internet the other day about Westerners making sure their children are self-sufficient financially when they grow up. It makes sense, otherwise our kids will never learn to be independent. You need to let your children have a taste of a poor life. That way they will cherish a better life when they grow up. If you give them too much money they will take everything for granted. We are poisoning our children by providing them with everything.

It is Friday. The grandparents have taken the children to the clinic.
They are concerned about the little girl.
Little sister's not feeling well, says grandfather. She's not laughing.
No, not laughing today, says the genial butcher.
Her little legs are sore after the injection, says grandmother.
Has she got a temperature? asks grandfather.
No, says the genial butcher, it's normal to feel sleepy after the injection.

Three Chinese women are standing by the windowsill. They are in their seventies, with grey hair combed behind their ears, neat and tight. They all dress in a similar style and colour, black shoes and black trousers. They are chatting in Cantonese. After a few minutes a Chinese man in his seventies walks towards the group. He opens his arms wide when he sees them, as if he wants to hug them all. The women are happy to see him as well. They greet each other loudly, with familiar pats on shoulders and backs. He tells them that as soon as he got their phone call he came to meet them. They chat for a while and walk out of the market together, heading across the road towards the restaurants in China Town.

The pragmatic butcher and the genial butcher are at home, looking at a website which advertises property for sale and rent. They discuss the possibility of buying a house so that they can rent it in the private letting market.
Wolverhampton, says the genial butcher, house prices in Wolverhampton are so cheap.
The pragmatic butcher is interested. Wolverhampton? he says, how much are the house prices?
Terraced houses are sixty to sixty-five thousand, she says.
But you can't compare Wolverhampton to the area around the university, he says, where there is far more potential for growth in house prices.

There's one here, says the genial butcher. It's very cheap. It's in an Asian area, and needs refurbishing.

The pragmatic butcher says the carpets also need changing.

He notices another property. How much is this?

B8. From forty-five thousand to forty-eight thousand, says the genial butcher.

Maybe if it's forty-five thousand, says the pragmatic butcher.

The genial butcher interrupts, saying bidding starts at forty-four, and there will be other bidders.

Is this an auction?

It's a house for auction, she says, let's see how much the bidders offer. If the bidding price comes to eighty thousand it will be too much for us, because it needs refurbishing. Indians often buy houses for refurbishing.

The pragmatic butcher looks at another property; this one costs fifty thousand, so it would still be profitable if we rent it out.

The genial butcher agrees.

But, he says, if it's in an Asian area we can't set the rent too high.

THE MAN ON THE NAILS AND BEAUTY STALL. This business is about nails and threading and waxing, this whole bodies and all that, once the customers go anywhere, if they like it, they don't want to go nowhere else. The same as with hairdressers. I've got a hairdresser for four years, just one place. Whether he's busy or not, I always go back. It's the same thing. It's okay. We can't be millionaires but at the end, it's okay. We don't want to be millionaires. It's okay. Eating bread and butter nicely, morning and evening. I have a five-year-old son, drop him at school. Afternoon I go, pick him up, he plays for about one hour, one hour and a half, market stops, we go home. So, from all sides, we are happy. Sometimes, in one week, two days or three days business, three days quiet, three days are busy, three days quiet. So when they're here for the rag market. On Wednesday the rag market is closed, so our business is quiet. If you come on Friday and Saturday, you can see a lot of people are here. Yes. So the first week is just okay. The second week is quiet. The third week is fully dead. The fourth week is very good. Why? Because people get paid at the end of the month. So the fourth week is very busy. First week is not that busy, but just okay busy. Second week goes a lot down, fifty per cent. The third week is very dead, but in one whole month, if we make our budget, as bread and butter, rent for this or any expenses, we are making something.

A Chinese man hurries by and gives the pork butcher from Enoch's a giant bar of Cadbury Dairy Milk chocolate. The butcher takes the giant bar of chocolate with a smile, waving to the Chinese man as he continues on his way through the market hall.

THE PORK BUTCHER. I went into hospital last week and it was a learning curve. I hadn't been into a hospital for thirty years. So I'm thinking in the dark ages, and I see these nurses running around like there's no tomorrow; they're under extreme pressure, looking after my needs, and I'm fast-tracking through all these departments just to have a routine check. You had this black nurse came up to me and she was going to give me an injection, she had to do this. I thought, well, if I get on the wrong side of her I've got a problem. So straight away I try to get into that person, talk to them. By the end of the day, and I was there from one o'clock to half past six, right, she was like a mother. She was telling me all sorts. She even went out and made me a cup of tea because I'd had nothing to eat, and gave me a packet of biscuits. If you're faceless or you don't talk, you're going to get this all the time. This is the problem with a lot of things in life. We don't mix and we're losing the art of that. The same as iPads and phones and texting. We're losing that art. At least here, I'm on the stage. That's what it's all about. There are days when you're absolutely worn out, knackered, but you've got to come here and you've got to do it, because the customers can pick up on it. I always try and say, if I've got a customer what looks scared or fed up, I try and make their day. Probably, you're the only person they're going to see. So they can go away and they've got that. Especially the old ones. They're there and they're talking to you, all this. It's all a part of connecting.

The pragmatic butcher is sitting cross-legged on the windowsill, his usual place for lunch. He has his lunch box and a bottle of drink. While he's eating a woman stops and peers into his lunch box.
Wow, smells nice, she says, what do you have there? The woman seems to know him well.
Dumplings and leftovers, the pragmatic butcher laughs.
Wow, dumplings! Yum, the woman says. Did your wife make you dumplings? Lucky you!
No, he says, she doesn't know how to make them. I do, but I've got no time. She can make yuntun though.

Two days later the pragmatic butcher checks again on the progress of the Chinese-student butcher.

how are you now, getting better?
have you lost your virginity?

today I am going for a check-up

do you feel better?

not yet, I wanted it too

you need to use your initiative
start kissing her and it'll be done

it's getting better but I still can't move it
it hurts a lot every time I try to move my fingers
– with the cast and bandage on it's not easy to make a move

the cast is not on your dick
nor is it on your
how come it's not easy?

your logic is there
but why does it sound so weird?

The pragmatic butcher's father-in-law has been shopping for suitcases.
How many cases have you brought back? asks the pragmatic butcher.
Only one, and two more cases to be shipped out, says father-in-law.
You're going to ship two cases? Why don't you ship all the cases?
This one to be here, three to be shipped, says father-in-law. And I bought a TV.
You have already got a large-screen TV at home, why did you buy another one?
I don't want to compete with Wei to watch my favourite TV channel, says father-in-law. Sometimes I want to watch it, but he is watching something, and he gets angry if I don't let him watch it.
You can use the computer to watch TV, says the pragmatic butcher.
I don't know how to turn it on, says father-in-law.

At the dinner table the genial butcher suggests that they buy fish the next day.
How about mackerel? asks the pragmatic butcher.
No, it smells too strong, she says.
He reminds her that they used to often buy mackerel. How about salmon? he says.
Too much salmon is not good, says the genial butcher.
What about turbot, for steaming, he says.
No good, too many bones, and it's slippery, she says.
It tastes good, he says. You have strange taste.
You can get some for yourself, she says.
It's too big, he says, I can't eat it all on my own.

✒

How is your new assistant working out? asks the pragmatic butcher's father-in-law.
I fired him this afternoon, says the pragmatic butcher. He was no use. It was really busy on Saturday, there were so many customers, at first he was all right if I kept an eye on him, but when I wasn't standing over him he did virtually nothing.
All day, says the genial butcher, he was asking how much is this, how much is that. You don't have time.

I thought I'd give him one more day, says the pragmatic butcher, but really he's not good enough. This morning I bought a sausage-and-bacon sandwich for him, he just ate the two pieces of bread and threw away the rest. Not so much as a thank you.
Maybe he can't eat pork, says the genial butcher.
No, he can, it's not that. He can eat it, I asked him. Also sometimes I don't understand what he's saying. It's better to have someone who has done the job before.
Or at least knows the prices, she says.
I sometimes think, says the pragmatic butcher, even someone with thirty-five years' experience isn't going to be good enough. Are you able to work tomorrow? he asks her.
It's not that I can't do it, but I would prefer if you can get someone else to help out, she says.
It would be better if we didn't do so many deliveries, says the pragmatic butcher.
I could switch to part-time, maybe, only work on busy days, she says.

A small man in denim jeans and a black jacket comes to the stall. He is a friend of the pragmatic butcher. He too is from Fujian. He has just arrived in Birmingham. While the pragmatic butcher and the genial butcher are working, he asks them for help with finding somewhere to live, and with finding a school for his daughter. He does not know how to go about securing a mortgage in the UK.
There's a website, says the genial butcher, Halifax. Type in your salary and they will tell you how much money you can borrow.
Halifax?
Any bank will do, she says.
Go to their website, put in your salary, and they will give you an estimate of how much you can borrow. She suggests renting until they can find something long term.
Go to the Zoopla website, she says, and type in your range, from how much to how much, and see what it can find for you. She shows him her phone.
He is interested in a flat for rent. Something like this will be fine, he says. B30, is it close to where you live?
That's right, she says. These are flats. A town house is cheaper, and it is more expensive if you want a new property.
The small man in denim jeans and a black jacket says, I am okay with anything. But if my wife comes later and likes the look of a different property, we probably will have to buy that one.
The genial butcher says, it's totally up to you. You will have to have a look yourself.
My wife doesn't drive, says the man, and it would be a lot of trouble for her to walk the kids to school every day.

If you're in a flat you will have to go up and down. That is troublesome as well, says the genial butcher.
The pragmatic butcher has been listening, and shouts over to his friend, look for something close to the school then.

The genial butcher agrees, go and search on the internet, and find something close to the school. Google it online, property near your daughter's school.

The pragmatic butcher is busy cutting meat.

Leave the meat saw with me, says his wife, and go and help him.

The pragmatic butcher is not enthusiastic about this. Huh? I don't know how to search.

Just type in Birmingham, she says, and how much money.

You help him do it, says the pragmatic butcher. Help him to type in a few search words.

How about the travel agent across the road that sells flight tickets, says the friend, do they do this stuff as well?

Of course, says the genial butcher, they can find something for you.

The pragmatic butcher says, if you don't want a long walk, look for something near the school, that would be the best.

Anyway, they have rules that you need to live within several miles of the school you want to register your children with, says the genial butcher. Have you thought about which area you want to live in?

The pragmatic butcher says, Erdington is fine.

I haven't thought about it, says the man.

So which school do you like? asks the genial butcher.

He says he does not know the schools.

This is the same as we did to buy our house, says the pragmatic butcher.

Not exactly, says the genial butcher. You should tell him to note down the details of the property, so he can call the agent to arrange a viewing.

How will he know if it's close to the school or not?

It will be in the house profile, says the genial butcher. What we did was to find the house on the map first before arranging the viewing, didn't we? He'll have to make up his mind where he wants to live.

The man thanks them and leaves.

The genial butcher tells him to let them know if he needs more help.

Will he get a place in the school? asks the pragmatic butcher.

He should do, says the genial butcher. If you live close to the school you can start in the middle of the term, as long as they have places.

An old man is resting against the windowsill. He is in his seventies, and frequently turns his head from side to side. A woman fishmonger in a white coat and hat walks past him, stops, walks back towards the man and says, hello, how are you? How nice to see you! She pats the man on the shoulder, smiling at him warmly. The man is very happy to see her. He chats to her for several minutes.

The pragmatic butcher speaks to a group of customers, moving between Cantonese, Mandarin, Hakka and the South Fujian dialect. He greets them like old friends. The stall is full of laughter and loud Chinese voices.

A Chinese man in a tweed jacket stops by the stall to talk to the butcher.
Your business is pretty good these days.
Just so so, says the pragmatic butcher.
My friends tell me you are doing really well, says the man.
Well, if that's what people say, says the pragmatic butcher. You're out shopping early today. Are you going to work?
Oh no, says the Chinese man in a tweed jacket, I start work at four and finish at eleven.
So seven hours, says the pragmatic butcher.
Yes, seven hours a day.
Or nearly eight hours by the time you've done the washing up, says the pragmatic butcher.
No, no, I leave at exactly eleven.
You are able to leave on time? So all the washing up has been done by then?
The kitchen helps finish up. I can go on time. The man laughs. They use a dishwasher now, which is really quick. It's not like it used to be when I had to work so hard. When I started I had to work myself to the bone to earn a hundred and seventy pounds a week.
The pragmatic butcher empathises, yes, about twelve hours a day.
But you must have been fed up with working in take-aways when you got out to set up your own business, says the Chinese man in a tweed jacket
I was totally stuffed, says the pragmatic butcher. How many years had I done? Ten years. I had been in it for ten years.
I have been doing it for eleven years now, laughs the man.
Aren't you fed up with it? asks the pragmatic butcher.
Fed up? I can't stand it anymore. Not like you, you have your own business. I have no choice but to get on with it.
That's what you have to do to feed hungry mouths, says the pragmatic butcher. When you have kids and family you have to stick with it, you can't just give it up. Am I right?
It's true. You are the capable one though, you got out.
Sometimes you need a bit of luck, says the pragmatic butcher.
You do need luck, says the man. They all say that you have bought quite a few houses already, in Solihull.
The pragmatic butcher laughs, Solihull? Who says? It's not true, he protests.
All your 老乡 said so, the Chinese man in a tweed jacket laughing at the pragmatic butcher's protests.
Oh, no, Solihull? I don't live there. The houses are so expensive there.
The man laughs again, and says no more.

The pragmatic butcher is helping his young daughter with her school work. This is add, this is subtract, that is take away, okay, do it over here.

The pragmatic butcher's daughter says, Dad, five take away five is five.

He corrects her, this is five minus five, you have five apples and you ate five, um, how many apples left?

Five, says the young student.

The teacher persists with the lesson, you have eaten five apples, they are in your stomach, you still have five?

She ventures another solution. Six.

How can you have more after you have eaten them?

But the student is in playful mood, seven eight nine ten eleven twelve.

The master has no time for such frivolity. I don't want to talk to you, you are silly, you think you have more apples after you have eaten them.

Having pushed her father to the point of irritation, the scholar knows when to produce the correct answer, and says, zero.

Satisfied, the teacher confirms, yes, you have eaten five, nothing left, that is zero, isn't it?

要多少? asks the pragmatic butcher. A Chinese couple is surprised but pleased to hear the butcher speaking Mandarin. They order pork, and when the butcher tells them the price the man offers coins to him, displaying them in the palm of his hand, asking the pragmatic butcher to take what he needs. 这个是十跑 says the butcher, 这个是二十的, pointing out the ten-pence and twenty-pence coins. 红色的都很小的 He tells them the small brown coins have little value. The couple leave, thanking the pragmatic butcher for his kindness.

The genial butcher is encouraging her father to buy a new phone.

Dad, she says, that Nokia phone, the one with no headset, the price has dropped, it was sixty pounds, now it's thirty.

Her mother agrees that thirty pounds is a good price.

The headset is just one pound from the Pound Shop, says the genial butcher.

But her father is resistant. Sometimes with that sort of thing you don't know when is the best time to buy. It's Nokia. Aren't there any Chinese phones?

Let me see, says the genial butcher.

Is it thirty pounds including the SIM card? asks her father.

The pragmatic butcher is tired at the end of the working day. He didn't sleep well last night. The baby was crying all night long. He complains that the long hours working on the stall are exhausting. But my English is so poor, he says, that this lousy job is the only thing I can do.

An old woman walks slowly towards the windowsill with the help of her grand-daughter. She sits down in stages.

There you go, Nan, we'll wait here for the car. The granddaughter holds the old woman's arms as she sits down. You all right here? she asks.

The old woman nods, I'm fine.

Do you want a Fanta? asks the younger woman.

Oh yes, says Nan, I'd like that. Get one for yourself as well.

The young woman leaves, and comes back in a few minutes with a can of drink. She passes it over to her nan.

You don't have one for yourself?

No, I'm okay. The young woman shakes her head and looks out of the window to the street. Soon a big silver car stops in front of the market entrance. The granddaughter holds her nan's arms with one hand, the other hand on her shoulder to keep her steady. They walk slowly out of the market, get into the car and are away.

For the genial butcher, getting her daughter to school is difficult. She holds the middle child in her arms. He doesn't want to go. The baby is in the pushchair. She hardly has the strength to hold the middle child and at the same time push the buggy.

Her mother tells her to leave early to avoid the school-run traffic. Get there by eight fifteen or eight twenty, she says.

The genial butcher doesn't know how she will be able to take the children. She also has to help out on the stall. They are short of staff again.

Her mother says she should help with the stall when the children are asleep.

Just like before, says the genial butcher, when she had to take her son to the stall while she was working. There was nobody to take care of him, so either she was selling and the pragmatic butcher was pushing him around the market in the pushchair, or vice versa. One selling and the other pushing. Sometimes he would sleep for a couple of hours, but never more than that. There was only the pragmatic butcher and her on the stall. She doesn't want to go back to that.

The genial butcher tells her mother that her father will help with deliveries on the market stall the next day.

He will go along and learn where to deliver. I hope he will be able to push the trolley, she says, it can be quite heavy.

Her mother says that he is strong enough, but he will need someone to show him where to go.

He will be on his own when he's on deliveries, says the genial butcher.
Her mother is not worried. It's nearby, isn't it?
Yes, in China Town.
If he can't do it in one go, he can do two rounds, says her mother.
The genial butcher smiles, he is on probation tomorrow then.
How heavy is the meat? asks her mother.
Ten kilos or so.
Like a bag of rice, says her mother.
Or it could be about fifteen kilos, sometimes more, eighteen, nineteen, maybe twenty kilos.
Is Wednesday a busy day for deliveries? asks her mother.
Yes, says the genial butcher.

She is quite stubborn now
she's growing up and has learned
how to throw a tantrum
she screams and slams the door
then starts crying

she's a strong character
haha the little one has long eye lines
so she won't have small eyes
when she grows up

she has small eyes
little sis is called Lijia Chen

Lijia sounds like a boy's name
what about her English name?

we haven't decided yet

what about the word meaning beauty
for a girl's name

little sis was born at home
so we chose Jia for home
it will sound like a girl's name
people can only tell if you write it
in Chinese

The genial butcher teaches her father how to watch online videos on his mobile phone. What do you want to watch? she asks.
What can you watch, anything? asks her father.
News, she says, *Guang Ming Daily*, Singapore daily newspaper.
Current or back-dated?
Current, she says.

Local or Malaysian?
Singapore Daily is Malaysian, she says.
Any drama?
Yes, on YouTube. See, *Singapore Daily*, can you see? She shows him on the mobile phone. Main news. Can you see? she asks.
Yes, says her father.
You can watch videos on YouTube. Which song you like? Deng Li Jun?
Shall I type the name?
Yes, but you can only watch if you have internet access.

The family discusses the possible purchase of a pixiu, made of jade, which has mythical power to bring wealth and fortune.
The genial butcher's mother suggests that they look for one next week.
But, her father says, they are very expensive.
We will buy it if they are a hundred pounds each, or two hundred for two, says the genial butcher, but they're not worth a thousand for two.
Her father says they should buy one if it really helps to increase their wealth, even if it is a thousand pounds for two.
The genial butcher looks for the price on her smart phone. Fifteen hundred, she says.
See if they will lower the price, says her mother.
It's too expensive, says the genial butcher, fifteen hundred pounds, even if they reduce it to a thousand, it's not worth it.
The pixiu has three legs, says her father.
The genial butcher disagrees, no, it's not three-legged.
It's the king of all animals, says her father, and they should be frightened.
The genial butcher reads from her phone. It says pixiu is a fierce, auspicious animal, it swallows everything without ever expelling anything.
It means keeping the wealth in, says her mother.
The genial butcher reads, it's capable of drawing wealth from all directions, warding off evil spirits and bringing good fortune.

The genial butcher is looking at a property website on her mobile phone. Highgate, B5, she says, one hundred thousand, a car park.
A car park? Is that worth buying? asks the pragmatic butcher.
It's B5, in the city centre, she says.
Is it city council?
No, she says, if you apply for specific use of the land you have to call the city council.
Where is it? he asks.
Bradford Street, says the genial butcher.
The pragmatic butcher is not convinced. If you think it's good, everybody will think it's good too, so the bidding will be high. But he supports her. Shall we try?

PART THREE

Bread

As before, nine wooden chairs face inwards in a circle. On the chairs sit THE PRAGMATIC BUTCHER, THE GENIAL BUTCHER, THE DRAMATURG, THE DOCUMENTARY NOVELIST, THE ENTRE-PRENEUR, THE PHOTOGRAPHER, THE POET, THE PROFESSOR *and* THE RESEARCHER.

THE GENIAL BUTCHER. We can only stay a couple more minutes. We have to pick up the kids.

THE RESEARCHER. Of course, of course, whenever you need to go.

THE POET. Yes, yes, no need to stay. You have already done so much.

THE PRAGMATIC BUTCHER. We're all right for a minute or two. We'll just go when we have to.

THE RESEARCHER. Well, I don't mind kicking off. I really like the way the voices sit alongside each other. *[To* THE DRAMATURG*]* It is exactly what you were describing, that thing about unfinalised and unfinished, different perspectives, no need for explanation, just the thing itself.

THE DRAMATURG. Yes, yes, that sense of separate voices coming together to form a coherent, collective whole. It is a good example of that. The fact that the different voices stand on their own, without an account of what they mean, and often without narrative, so that the listener, or the reader, the audience, can bring a critical orientation to them. That is what we aim for. To provide an opportunity for critical reflection on social life.

THE POET. What I picked up was how intimate it felt, listening in to these voices, these conversations, these relationships. I mean at times we were at someone's dinner table, private family time. Incredibly intimate. It was almost intrusive at times, but not quite, because it also felt like it was consensual. I mean, it wasn't like eavesdropping. The characters were involved in their own curation.

THE ENTREPRENEUR. But where's the story? Where's the hook? Isn't it all a bit repetitive and boring?

THE DRAMATURG. I would say that the representation of those voices, those perspectives, or world-views, of the various characters in the market, allows us to take a critical view of the kind of society we live in, and even of the kind of society we might aspire to live in, if that isn't putting it too grandly. I mean, the life of the market is the life of society, with all its pressures and tensions, but also with all its small ceremonies of courtesy and conviviality. I think that's what it is.

The photographer. Yes it's those small moments, the moments of interaction between strangers, when people overcome their differences, or their potential differences, and get on with getting on with each other. It's what I have called nothing very much. Well, it's nothing very much, but it is also the whole world. It is the universal in the mundane. It is a manifestation of how social life works in spite of everything.

The documentary novelist. And more than that. It isn't always about people's differences being a problem. In fact, differences between people can be ignored, but at the same time they can be a resource. They can be the very means by which people manage to rub along together. The characters in the market say, oh, where are you from, which language do you speak, that's interesting, we're all from somewhere else, so in a sense we're all the same.

The poet. Yes, I think that's it exactly. And what we see again and again is that it isn't about separate individuals coming together, so much as the relationship itself that we should be thinking about. That space in which both or all of those concerned invest in that momentary encounter. What happens in that space amounts to a relationship. That is where the work of social life goes on. I think I have learned that just by looking at what happens when people interact in the market.

The photographer. But we have to be sure that, as outsiders, we do not run away with a romantic view of social interaction in the market. In the end, for the traders the work is hard, even if it has a convivial element to it. And there is discrimination, there is racism, there is a scrap for resources. The market is not always one big, happy family. It can be a tough place to work. Just because it looks like a superdiverse, multicultural environment, that doesn't wash away the tension or the competition. Everyone has to make a living.

The professor. We always try to be aware of that. I mean it's definitely a danger. We try to show the world as it is, warts and all. But we have still had to make some difficult decisions about what we left out of the final version. Some of the less palatable aspects of life in the market did not make the final cut. There's a balance to be found. On the one hand, we wanted to represent everything we saw. On the other hand, we did not want to give oxygen to some instances of what you might call Billingsgate discourse. There were examples of misogynistic talk, and racist talk, which we decided to omit. Is that censorship? I'm not sure. Do we end up with a romantic view of the life of the market? A sanitised view? Possibly. Is it, then, more difficult for the audience to take a critical perspective? I don't know. The team didn't always agree about what should be included or omitted. We reached compromises through discussion. It's about checks and balances. You want to show the world as it is, but you don't want to offend. It is not an exact science.

THE RESEARCHER. I don't disagree. But if you don't mind me saying, what I found is missing is something of the broader research process, or rather something of the way the research team worked together. You know, this work was done over several years, and in multiple locations, in several cities. A lot of the collaborative work involved in developing the ideas is backgrounded here. Other voices in the team were important in shaping the ideas that contributed to this.

THE PROFESSOR. At risk of being defensive, I think it is difficult to separate out the contributions of everyone in the research team. People contributed in different ways. Everyone's voice is valued. It's difficult to always say this idea belongs to this individual. Accepting the notion of a collective view is a by-product of doing collaborative work. Hopefully we speak with one voice, which is imbued with multiple voices. We tried to work in a democratic, egalitarian way at all times.

THE POET. But who gets to decide which voices go forward? In the end, it is difficult to involve everyone in every decision. There is bound to be a hierarchy. It is in the nature of teams. Someone is ultimately responsible. So someone assumes greater power than others.

THE DRAMATURG. That is probably inevitable. Otherwise things don't get done. But one of the noticeable things about this work is that it is such a collective effort. I agree that there is a danger in the final product that some of the contributions are erased, or at least, if not erased, backgrounded. Is that inevitable? It's an interesting point. In the theatre, does the stage hand take the plaudits at the curtain call? Does the props manager, the understudy, the prompt, the box office clerk? For that matter, does the dramaturg? Each is essential in their own way, but they are not all made for the spotlight. They are all members of the team that makes the show a success. It's that sense of collective endeavour, you might say collective action.

THE RESEARCHER. That is true. But we can't precisely transpose the model of the theatre to the research team. It may be that the theatre is always going to be hierarchical.

THE DRAMATURG. I'm not sure that theatre companies are inevitably hierarchical. We should hang on to the possibility of a theatre that is truly collective, a theatre that values the voice of everyone.

THE POET. Do you think you achieved your aim, that you ran the project in a democratic way? If you did, all kudos and praise to you! Your project might be last bastion of egalitarian practice. The last outpost, as one of your butchers might say!

THE RESEARCHER. As far as possible, yes, I think we did. Although I would admit that sometimes it was more difficult than at other times.

THE PHOTOGRAPHER. But in terms of power relations? What about gender, and the question of whose voice was heard?

THE PROFESSOR. It's a good question. We asked everyone in the team to write a reflective piece on their role in the team. We have that, so we can give an account from the perspective of each team member. All I can say is that there was a real effort there to run things in a fair way. Did some of the senior, white male academics do most of the talking in some of the meetings? I wouldn't be surprised if they did. We recorded the meetings, so we can do that analysis. But we made a conscious effort to make sure that everyone had a voice, and that each voice could be heard.

THE PRAGMATIC BUTCHER. What about the voices of the research participants?

THE ENTREPRENEUR. Yes, another good question!

THE PHOTOGRAPHER. Well, we can surely see that the voices of the butchers are very much in evidence here. They are not backgrounded at all. But for me, these are questions once again of curation. The issue of whether other voices from the research team make the final cut is about who selects the material, and how that selection is made, and why. The work here has been curated in a particular way, removing explanation and analysis, leaving the original material intact. That might mean that some of the ideas are implicit rather than explicit. But I approve of that. It is exactly what I have been trying to do in my own work. Letting the thing stand for itself. Letting the material speak for itself. It is risky, but I think it succeeds.

THE POET. The other thing is that even when you say that the material speaks for itself, it always bears the traces of its making. What was it you said? Like the finger marks of the sculptor still visible in the final piece of work, or the artist's cartoon hidden but always there, beneath the oil painting. It's something like that. That dialogic thing. Every voice shaped by other voices. So the wider research team, your thirty-odd people, are all part of the shaping of the piece, part of the making of the overall research outcome.

THE RESEARCHER. I still worry. It's all right for the senior people, but others need to be given credit for their role in the team. We can't assume that all members of the team have the same needs. It's about different relations of power. The way universities are now, with so much pressure on junior academics, we should be diligent about crediting their achievements.

THE GENIAL BUTCHER. I don't think we met all the other people in the team, did we? What was their role? How did they contribute?

THE PROFESSOR. The team was spread across six universities, with academic researchers in each university working on the project. As you know, we are interested in the way people communicate when they have different backgrounds and different languages. So we looked at the national census and worked out which were the main languages spoken in the inner-city wards where we were doing the research. And we recruited researchers who spoke those different languages – Polish, Czech, Romani, Slovak, Arabic, Portuguese, Mandarin, Cantonese – and who had the skills and experience to do ethnographic field work in particular city communities. The project was interdisciplinary. That is, we wanted to look at a wide range of city contexts, including businesses, the cultural heritage sector, sports clubs, and legal and welfare advice settings. So we included in the research team expert academics in those areas. And then we recruited partners who were not working in academic institutions, but were interested in the questions we were asking. They included museums, libraries, sports organisations, legal advice networks, migrant support groups. All of these partners came to meetings, ran dissemination events and contributed in all sorts of ways. And, as I was saying, we collaborated with artists, including a theatre company, a composer, a choreographer, a street artist and a curator. They not only made the research accessible to a wider constituency of the public, but also expanded our understandings of the research itself, as they came at it with new, more creative eyes. So all these different types of expertise became part of the research team. It was an incredibly rich experience to be part of. Finding ways for such a large and complex team to work together, and ensuring that we got the best out of everyone, and making certain that the result of the collaboration was more than the sum of its very considerable parts, was a challenging task.

THE GENIAL BUTCHER. We didn't see all those people down here at the market, did we?

THE RESEARCHER. In fact some of them did visit the market once or twice. We brought the artists down here, and the people from the museums. But, by then, we felt that you had been under the microscope enough, so we didn't disturb you.

THE PRAGMATIC BUTCHER. So did you say you did the same kind of research in other meat and fish markets in other cities, is that it?

THE RESEARCHER. Not exactly in markets. Well, kind of. We wanted to look at small businesses in each city, and to examine how people communicate in those contexts. How people communicate when there is that commercial imperative. In fact in the other cities we ended up looking at a Polish shop and an Arabic shop. So they weren't very different from the market stall in some respects. Probably your market stall attracted a greater diversity of customers, in terms of people from different ethnic and national backgrounds. [To THE GENIAL BUTCHER] What was it you said – in the market you can catch all kinds of fish? It was that diversity of the market that interested us. People coming together from all sorts of different origins and backgrounds.

THE ENTREPRENEUR. You see people in the market with different histories, and from different places, but it is not a comprehensive spread. You probably miss certain social categories. The well-off, the middle classes if you like, are less likely to shop in the market. Not everyone goes to the market.

THE RESEARCHER. Well, yes, that's probably true. I'm not sure that class divisions are so straightforwardly identifiable now. But no, there are people who would never shop in the market.

THE PRAGMATIC BUTCHER. You did the same kind of thing in the other cities, then, writing notes, making recordings, interviews, copying digital messages, everything else?

THE PROFESSOR. Yes, exactly. We used the same model across all sixteen research sites.

THE GENIAL BUTCHER. Sixteen!

THE RESEARCHER. And so you can imagine how much material we collected. What we did at your butcher's stall you can multiply sixteen times. If anything, it was too much. It ran to more than a million words of field notes alone, never mind the transcripts. You get to the point where you can't ever analyse everything in detail.

THE PRAGMATIC BUTCHER. It sounds like it's a lot of studying.

THE PROFESSOR. And that's why you need a team of people who trust each other. When you have that trust, people will work together, go the extra mile for each other. The other thing was that the team itself was quite diverse, ethnically, linguistically, socially. That was one of its strengths.

THE ENTREPRENEUR. If this was a commercial enterprise, you would have turned your success into profit. Aren't you missing a trick? Shouldn't you be making money out of this so that you can invest in other research in future?

THE RESEARCHER. That is not what it is about. It's about advancing knowledge. Making a contribution, pushing at the already known, reaching into the previously unknown. Discovering something original. We know some things about social interaction in the cities of the twenty-first century that we didn't know before. Isn't that enough?

THE ENTREPRENEUR. That's all very worthy and laudable, I'm sure. Knowledge is a good thing. But does it put bread on the table? You have done thousands of hours of work, as far as I can see it is high-quality work, but you have not made a profit. In business that would be called failure. You would be out on your ear. The only thing that matters is the bottom line. I thought universities had moved to a business model these days. I can't see it here. Your work is highly marketable. But all you do is sit around and talk about it. There's a marketplace out there.

THE DRAMATURG. They are not in the business of commodifying knowledge. Not everything is about marketisation. Not everything is about turning a profit.

THE PRAGMATIC BUTCHER. Isn't it? In the end, what else counts? Above all else, we have to eat.

THE GENIAL BUTCHER. You know, he's right. At the end of the day, you have to put bread on the table.

THE ENTREPRENEUR. In the real world, in the world as it is, I'm afraid that is what counts. You heard it from the people who matter. All of this energy and industry, all of this brain power, must lead to something tangible, something that has an actual value. In the end, business is business. If you have created a quality product, you have a responsibility to market it. It's a no-brainer. You can't live in an imaginary world where knowledge has a value that is separate from the prevailing economic model. That model determines everything. If your product is better than the next person's product, you are entitled to profit from it. That is what competition is about. That is what the market is about. That is how the world moves forward. Without competition there would be no progress. When you apply for research funding it is all about competition, isn't it? Your proposal is better than the next professor's proposal. So you win. Competition provides better products and innovation, creates strong economic growth, and yields productivity and prosperity that benefits society. That is it: price, product, distribution, promotion. And so the wheels go round. Buyers compete with buyers. Sellers compete with sellers. That is the way the world works. Have you got something that other people want? Put it on the market. Have you got something that other people need? Do not sell it cheaply. Get the highest price you can. That is the game. That is when you know you have succeeded. That is when you are winning. Look at the meat and fish market. Do you think any of those butchers and fishmongers would be there in the draughty market hall from six in the morning to six at night, six days a week, if they were not turning a profit? Keep wages low. Sell for what you can get. But above all, stay ahead of the competition. That is what we learn from the market.

THE PROFESSOR. That is not what we set out to do. We push at the borders of the already known. We generate new knowledge. And we will give that knowledge freely, for the advancement and improvement of the world. That is enough. That is more than enough.

THE GENIAL BUTCHER. Look, I'm sorry, but we need to go. My parents will be getting anxious. We're late to get the kids. It's been very interesting. Thank you.

THE PHOTOGRAPHER. No, thank you, thank you both. Good bye, good bye.

THE PRAGMATIC BUTCHER. It's been nice to meet you all. Good bye. [To THE RE-SEARCHER] About the expenses, do you have a … ?

THE RESEARCHER. Yes, yes, of course. I'll go out with you. Thank you so much for coming. I'll see to it. After you, please.

Notes

(1) This work was supported by the Arts and Humanities Research Council (1 April 2014–31 March 2018) through a Translating Cultures Large Grant: 'Translation and Translanguaging. Investigating Linguistic and Cultural Transformations in Superdiverse Wards in Four UK Cities' (AH/L007096/1; £1,973,527), Principal Investigator, Angela Creese. With Mike Baynham, Adrian Blackledge, Jessica Bradley, John Callaghan, Lisa Goodson, Ian Grosvenor, Amal Hallak, Jolana Hanusova, Rachel Hu, Li Wei, Agnieszka Lyons, Bharat Malkani, Sarah Martin, Emilee Moore De Luca, Jenny Phillimore, Mike Robinson, Frances Rock, James Simpson, Caroline Tagg, Jaspreet Kaur Takhi, Janice Thompson, Kiran Trehan, Piotr Wegorowski and Zhu Hua.

(2) Other publications which refer to the material presented here include the following:

Blackledge, A. and Creese, A. (2018) Interaction ritual and the body in a city meat market. *Social Semiotics* (DOI 10.1080/10350330.2018.1521355).

Blackledge, A. and Creese, A. (2018) Language and superdiversity. An interdisciplinary perspective. In A. Creese and A. Blackledge (eds) *The Routledge Handbook of Language and Superdiversity* (pp. xxi–xlv). London: Routledge.

Blackledge, A. and Trehan, K. (2018) Language, superdiversity, and self-employment. In A. Creese and A. Blackledge (eds) *The Routledge Handbook of Language and Superdiversity* (pp. 299–311). London: Routledge.

Blackledge, A. and Creese, A. (2017) Translanguaging and the body. *International Journal of Multilingualism* 14 (3), 250–268 (DOI 10.1080/14790718.2017.1315809).

Blackledge, A. and Creese, A. (2017) Language education and multilingualism. In T. McCarty and S. May (eds) *Language Policy and Political Issues in Education* (pp. 73–84). *Encyclopedia of Language and Education* (3rd edn). New York: Springer, Cham (DOI 10.1007/978-3-319-02320-5_6-1).

Blackledge, A. and Creese, A. (2017) Translanguaging in mobility. In S. Canagarajah (ed.) *The Routledge Handbook of Migration and Language* (pp. 31–46). London: Routledge.

Blackledge, A., Creese, A. and Hu, R. (2017) Everyday encounters in the marketplace: Translanguaging in the super-diverse city. In A. De Fina, D. Ikizoglu and J. Wegner (eds) *Diversity and Super-Diversity: Sociocultural Linguistic Perspectives* (pp. 97–116). Washington, DC: Georgetown University Press.

Blackledge, A., Creese, A. and Hu, R. (2016) The structure of everyday narrative in a city market. *Journal of Sociolinguistics* 20 (5), 654–676.

Blackledge, A., Creese, A. and Hu, R. (2015) *Voice and Social Relations in a City Market*. Working Papers in Translanguaging and Translation (WP2), available at https://tlang754703143.files.wordpress.com/2018/08/voice-and-social-relations-in-a-city-market.pdf.

Creese, A., Blackledge, A. and Hu, R. (2018) Translanguaging and translation: The construction of social difference across city spaces. *International Journal of Bilingual Education and Bilingualism* 21 (7), 841–852, available at https://www.tandfonline.com/doi/full/10.1080/13670050.2017.1323445.

(3) A short film produced as an outcome of the research conducted in the market is available at https://www.youtube.com/watch?v=Ea1rPkt82ms.

(4)   Further information about the wider research project is available at https://www.birmingham.ac.uk/generic/tlang/about/index.aspx.

(5)   The epigraphs (p. v) are taken from the following sources:

Aleksievich, S. (2016) *On the Battle Lost*. Nobel Lecture, available at https://www.nobelprize.org/prizes/literature/2015/alexievich/lecture.

Brecht, B. (1965 [1963]) *The Messingkauf Dialogues*. Trans. John Willett. London: Methuen.

Lange, D. (1965) *Under the Trees*. KQED for National Educational Television (NET).

Paterson, D. (2018) *The Poem*. London: Faber.

These sources inform the speech of THE DOCUMENTARY NOVELIST, THE DRAMATURG, THE PHOTOGRAPHER and THE POET.

(6)   All photographs are by Joel Blackledge.

(7)   With grateful thanks to Rachel Hu, without whose unstinting work, enthusiasm and insight this book would not have been possible.